STOP DRIVING
BEHIND
IDIOTS

Leadership Systems for
Breakthrough Performance

By

Walt Carter & John Vinyard

"The greatest driver of all is the one who drives for himself, stays out of the idiot's way and wins."
Mario Andretti

Gratitude

The authors are grateful to Prince William County Water in Woodbridge, Virginia for allowing us to use their Leadership System as the model for this book. Hopefully this will inspire you to develop your own approach to systematic leadership.

Thank You

> *"It's not just about what we accomplish, but how we get there. Strong leaders create a culture where people can thrive. They mentor, inspire, create a sense of purpose, and champion a positive work environment where an employee's health, well-being, and belonging are valued."*
>
> *Calvin Farr*
> *General Manager & CEO*
> *Prince William Water*

Contents

Foreword: From Boeing's Heyday

By E. David Spong

The first few chapters of this book provide background, rationale, and justification for a leadership system--an important tool for a high performing organization.

I remember the first time I heard of a leadership system was when I was with the McDonnell-Douglas C-17 Program, based in Long Beach, CA. We were utilizing the Malcolm Baldrige Principles to improve.

As I remember one of the criteria instructions was, "Describe your Leadership System." We had no clue as to what a leadership system was. Our solution was to ask ourselves, "What do we do, or maybe what should we be doing to execute our program well." We struggled with our answer for a while, going through many iterations and finally publishing something which we improved over the years.

Later, when I moved to lead the Boeing Aerospace organization in St Louis, MO our leadership team adopted the C-17 leadership system (with modifications of course)!

To our delight, the C-17 program was recognized with a Malcolm Baldrige National Quality Award in 1998. At the conference the following year (1999) I shared our approach to leadership, including our leadership system.

I was both surprised and delighted to see at the next year's conference (2000) Ritz Carlton, who was receiving their second Baldrige award, showing (what was very close to) the C-17 leadership system as theirs, and I am equally delighted to see the example leadership shown in the Chapters below, from the Prince William County Water in Prince William County, Virginia, is in essence the C-17 leadership system.

My sharing this story is not to brag about the C-17 leadership system, but rather to emphasize how useful a leadership system is for enabling a high performing organization.

Be careful, however, just having a diagram is only interesting. The real utility comes from incorporating all the tools and learning described in this book!

Lead on!

E. David Spong

What Leaders are saying
about the book:

This book reframes leadership as a system—rooted in character and powered by alignment between mission, vision, values, culture, and strategy. With vivid analogies and real-world examples, it transforms complex ideas into actionable insights for building stronger teams and more intentional organizations.

Tim Huff

CEO
Turknett Leadership Group

Stop Driving Behind Idiots is a refreshing and insightful take on leadership.

Does the world need yet another book on leadership? Absolutely. While leadership has been discussed for generations, mastering it remains as challenging as ever.

Authors Carter and Vinyard skillfully break down the key traits of exceptional leaders and, more importantly, provide actionable strategies to enhance leadership skills in clear, digestible steps. Their approach makes this book both engaging and practical.

I highly recommend *Stop Driving Behind Idiots* to anyone looking to grow as a leader and navigate the complexities of leadership with confidence.

Tino Mantella

President, Retained Executive Search

A wonderful collection of advice, stories, and (most importantly) frameworks to help anyone develop and leverage a leadership system—providing guidance, a *'measuring as you go'* approach, focus, and a method to *find and fill the gaps* every organization faces. Take the time to navigate and enjoy this particular journey with Walt and John. While you never know what you'll encounter along the road, having a meaningful leadership system will help you steer, accelerate, brake, and adjust your way to a successful, *values* (not merely value) *driven* organization.

Dr. Ken Russell

Co-Author of Transact Transform Transcend: Becoming a Thoughtful Leader

Dedication

This book, the experiences shared, the wisdom and the learning could not have occurred without constant love and support of our wives, Eileen Carter and JoAnn Vinyard. Their support has been pivotal.

Prologue

A conversation with David Spong
March 12, 2024

(David Spong, Walt Carter, and John Vinyard)

Walt: David, when you first took on this task of looking at the leadership criteria for Baldrige and were setting out to create a leadership system for your group, what were the major challenges, and what would you say were the biggest 'ah-has' on the other side after winning the Baldrige a couple of times?

David: I'm not sure I've an answer specifically but let me sort of walk around it.

   When McDonnell Douglas initially started their Baldrige journey, I think there were five divisions and each division was going to use it, not apply for an award. At least that's what the guidance was. But the headquarters was in St. Louis, and so they set up some people--I'll call them touchy-feely people, because I don't quite know how to explain it, to manage the program. Ken Best was one of them that John may remember. Each of us was assigned a section of the criteria to write a response to, and so I was assigned some section.

I would read a question. I divided the questions up into three buckets. The three buckets were: 1) I can read the question, 2) I can understand the question, and 3) I think I've got an answer. I probably didn't have an answer, but I thought I had an answer.

Then the next bucket was, I can read the question, I can understand the question, but I don't have a clue about the answer. The third bucket really was, I don't even understand the question, let alone have an answer. And so, I talked to Ken Best, who in a sense spoke a different language to me. I mean, I was all engineering, and he was all this improvement science stuff. He said, in essence, you will get it, but it was sort of a building block. You've got to work with it, move up the ladder, if you will, and then once you get a different perspective and you've got some of this stuff behind you, those questions will make more sense, and the answers will become evident to you.

And you know, as a scientist, I don't like that answer, but he was right. And after I'd been working at it for several years, I finally did understand all the questions. Not sure I always had a good answer, but at least I understood the questions. So that when we were applying the second time, and I was assigned part of the leadership section to write, I would read the question and I d go, "Oh, darn. We ought to be doing that. We aren't doing that. Let's do that and hope by the time the examiners get here, we've actually moved along, and we can show progress."

Obviously, we wouldn't be at the end. So, I kind of think that worked with the leadership system. We were struggling with, "What is a leadership system?" We came up with one, and then I'm not sure we used it in the sense of, you know, I'm building a house, I need a hammer and some nails, and I started using the hammer. No, I think we were still trying to figure out what the hammer was. But gradually, as it became evident what we were doing and what we weren't doing, and what we should be doing better. The maturity of the leadership system came in such that we could all talk to it. We all understood it in the sense that it was just a diagram, but it was something that enabled us to understand, "What are we doing today? What do we need to do today? And are we doing it? Are we measuring what we're doing?" So, I don't think it was a light bulb going on. It was a gradual maturation of understanding, just the same as with the criteria.

Walt: And when you built the second one, because my hypothesis is that you had a different leadership system, very similar to the first one, but different because of the different people at the second group, and you had been through a learning cycle...

What were the differences? And again, I believe that you probably did evolve, right? And so, did you start in a better place with the second group?

David: That's a good point. I then was to take over the group in St. Louis. As I mentioned earlier, each of the five divisions was supposed to have been using Baldrige, and of course in St. Louis, because they knew better-- they hadn't done anything! Here I walk in. I'm a card-carrying member of the Baldrige community. I've got this Baldrige win behind me. And these people really don't want anything to do with it. But they've got to do it because I'm the boss, right? I mean, I don't know whether all companies have it, but aerospace companies have a military style of organization.

Whatever the boss says he or she wants, the boss is going to get. Not always delivered well, but he's going to get it. So, I said we were going to have a leadership system, and we threw up the one that we'd had in

California, which to us who were there, there was maybe five of us, you know, worked, it was good.

Of course, the St. Louis people didn't like it. They didn't want it. But they settled down and argued and rephrased. I think the diagram per se with the central hub and the spokes around was the same. I think the one that we had initially was actually not circular but like in a rectangle.

And the one that we did at Aerospace Support, the second one, was more of an ellipse, like that makes any difference. So, I think most of the intent was still there, but it was just wordsmithing. That's the way I remember it. I don't think it was any better. But obviously by the senior leadership team building it, they ultimately had to take ownership of it, whether they wanted to or not. And we used the new design.

Walt: John and I talked about that, as really that word you used earlier on, the magic, is not so much, here's a leadership system, use it. It's, "Here's YOUR leadership system. Help us not only design it so that it works here, but so that it's internalized by the leaders." And I think that exercise is probably one of the more important parts of building into an organization is going through that, even though it feels like, well, we could just use the old one.

Again, my hypothesis. And by the way, David, I'm a physicist and my hypothesis is that if you don't go through that exercise and let them internalize, and make it their own, it won't ever seat correctly.

David: Exactly. I absolutely agree with you. And, you know, the other thing in your book, you've listed the aerospace support--What is it called? Leadership principles, John? Operating principles.

John: Operating principles are shown in the Appendix to this book.

David: And again, we did the same thing. We had a set in California. And again, we recreated it, not in my words, it was recreated in St. Louis and at our first offsite. And so it was now in words that that team had created. And I think we did make it better over time. I mean, for example, when Enron came around, we changed the first one to integrity is above all, which you can--we can all buy into. But, again, it was St. Louis's own, and we all had badge extenders. All aerospace companies at that time had picture badges for everyone. Then we put an extender behind it, which listed the operating principles.

We had them up on the wall in the conference room. When one of us broke them, as we did from time to time, typically the ones that people would break would be talking when the person in the front is talking, having a private conversation. Or even worse, answering a cell phone. And we would stop and stare at this person and often take off our badge extenders and flick them across the conference table at the offending person. And they got the message. And it was all done with a joke. But very soon, those behaviors stopped.

And you're living it, right? I mean, that's sort of what's going on. And as John will know, I've spoken all over the world, and given basically the same briefing to everybody, in China and Australia. And the one slide that everyone wants is the operating principles. That's the one. I've given it out all over the world. And I find that really interesting as to how powerful that is.

John: David, I'll make a comment about one of the principles, is the desire for velocity. I remember when you were in Long Beach, we went in and told you about a problem we had. We said, "David, you need to get this fixed. And if you can get it fixed within three weeks, it won't bite us. But if it goes longer than that, it is going to, it's going to hurt us."

I left your office, and I walked into Jay Kapmeyer's office right next door. And it was only a few minutes later, your assistant walks in and says, "it's fixed." I remember looking at her saying, I have no idea what's fixed. "The thing you told him he had three weeks on, he fixed in five minutes. He called Mr. X; he called Ms. Y; he called St. Louis; he talked to Mr. C; it's fixed."

David: Yes. And that is my mantra: Fix it now.

John: And in all of these things, processes are so key because if you leave the process behind, and IF your successor's smart, they will try to build on that and do things you didn't have time to do. If they're foolish, they'll try to do it all over again.

We worked with General Reimer when he was a four-star at Army Forces Command in Atlanta before he became Chief of Staff of the Army. General Reimer said, "Look, I have commanders change every two years, and you can look at the performance of a command in two-year cycles." But he went on to say, "I understand you'll have two-year cycles as the commanders change, but wouldn't it be nice if it was on a favorable improvement slope?"

Walt: I have another theory about your operating principles, and John and I have talked about this a lot, and it's kind of a core tenet in the book, is that old Drucker saying, well it's attributed to Drucker, I don't think he actually said it, but, "Culture eats strategy for breakfast."

Your operating principles define a culture that for most of us professionals, we're hoping to be part of a culture like that. That's the culture that we all feel safe in. A culture we feel like we can bring our best in. And I don't think great people or good people mind being held accountable to a high standard. It's actually the parasites and the weak folks that you don't want to have on your team anyway, that are always offended by those things.

And so, having a bias for action or velocity as you called it, to me, is a great thing. It's not a bad thing. I've got a watch that my team gave me and engraved on the back of it: "Full Turtle Power," because I say that a lot. Let's go forward. Let's go at full turtle power. Let's go as fast as a turtle can go. Let's make sure we're real deliberate about what we're doing. I have a bias for action, though, which is I'm going to go--I'm just going to go deliberately because you have another saying in the in the special ops part of the military that says, "Getting to smooth is slow. But smooth is fast." You have to move slowly first in order to build up the skills and I think your culture set a standard for excellence and how you were going to perform together, right? How we were going to work together in such a way that it enabled whatever your strategies or your goals or objectives were to get some coherence and some cohesive around it that would allow people to move with confidence.

David: Yeah, you're absolutely right. In hindsight, I think the real enabler was the culture that we created and sustained. There's a book on my shelf there somewhere called *The Rudolph Factor* by a young woman who spoke at one of our conferences one time. The reason it's called *The Rudolph Factor* is, she likened an organization to a bunch of people, often misfits in the organization, which would like to try things, do good things, but they're afraid to stick their heads up. And so, she likened it to turning their noses on and becoming like Rudolph the red-nosed reindeer. And anyway, that's written around the C-17 story.

I think I wrote a forward for that or an intro or something. I've forgotten. It's some time ago. But Just sort of to put the point to rest, in a sense, is I'm on LinkedIn, which you probably both are too. I use it for absolutely nothing because I don't work anymore. But every now and again, over the past two years in particular, I've been getting emails from people. And through LinkedIn asking to connect with me. I don't know what people think they're going to get out of connecting with me, but anyway, I always say yes.

But these days I ask, I say, "Yeah, I'm more than happy to be connected, but why do you want to connect?" And invariably they say, "I worked on the C-17, and you did such a great job." So that culture is something that they remember because, you know, most of them just saw me as, I'll say, a figurehead, but it was the culture that they were feeling. And I just find that incredibly powerful that people can recognize the culture, and you think, well, how did that get created? You know, obviously when you're talking, people hear you talk, but we know all sorts of politicians that talk and promise all sorts of things, and we don't believe any of it.

But somehow people get the culture, they FEEL the culture. And that is truly magic. I know the grapevine helps. But I find it hard to understand exactly why someone can create a culture and have everyone feel it. Because I would go to these 120 sites around the US, I would go to almost all of them. I didn't get to everyone, because some of them was just places where they pack spares for the Air Force. You know, they get materials in from their supplies, pack them up and send them to the various bases.

But I'd walk in, and they'd all know me. And I'd walk over to the bulletin board and there's my picture up with some pronouncement or other, but they felt it too. And I don't think we had anything at Minot (where Walt served in the Air Force), but we had them at some pretty far out places.

And I just think, you know, whoever said 'culture eats strategy for breakfast,' or whatever the exact quote was, got it right. It would be nice to be able to put a formula out that said: Follow this and it will all work. I don't quite know how to do that. I know how to create a culture, but it's more by gut than it is by anything else.

John: David, let me make a culture comment about what I saw with the operating principles.

As an outsider watching your group at Aerospace Support, I saw over not that much time, you know, six months, nine months, 12 months, but I saw in that group-- number one, you didn't hide a problem. You brought a problem up, and you could bring the ugliest, most difficult problems up, and that group would sit and look at it and unemotionally decide what they're going to do, and everybody would agree and then move it along and come to the next problem.

That was just a very powerful experience. I remember sitting with one of your executives and he had a really serious problem. He was talking about how he was going to make sure everybody knew it and what he was going to do about it because he owned it.

David: That's powerful. Yeah. In fact, I don't know if you remember, I used to talk kind of crudely about that stuff because I said, "You've got a problem. It's like a turd and you can try and sweep the turd under the carpet. Or you can put it in the center of the conference table and let's figure out how we're going to bronze it." And so that's the answer. And I was deliberately crude because I wanted to make an impact. And you're right--That was a key element in that whole thing.

John: It was wonderful to watch that leadership team as a group. Anyone would say, "If it is my problem, I'll bring it forth." Somebody may have a better idea about how to fix it. I'm all ears because I want to fix the problem. And it's real clear I own it. And that was really powerful because you had talented, talented people around there. And the minute they were going to start a blame game, that was going to go down the tubes.

David: Oh, yeah. And in fact, the Aerospace Support team had a lot of retired military people in it, mostly Air Force. So, they certainly understood the needs of the military customer. And I, in those last few years of work, I would get to work at six and I leave at 6:30. So, I was there when everyone else was there and a lot when they weren't. And every now and again, around six o'clock in the evening, I get a call from some airman on some base somewhere in the world and he wanted some help.

Of course, I couldn't help him, but my number was the general number that people could find. My secretary was going home, and I'd say, "I have no idea, but hold on, I will get on the other phone. I'm not trying to transfer you because I'll lose you. I'll get on the other line, and I'll find someone who can help you." And I would stay on that phone until I got someone who spoke that language, and then I'd connect the two of them.

Again, when you're a young, fresh-faced airman out there, someone actually stays on the line to help you. In the early days of C-17, we would patch the crew flying the airplane with a problem into the engineer that designed it, real time, and have him talk them through the issue. Usually, it was some avionics system that wouldn't reboot or something. But again, making that connection to the customer happen is very powerful. It is. It would even be powerful today.

Walt: Unfortunately, the truth of our existence as customers for a lot of these big companies is that it's almost impossible to get somebody on the phone now. Getting somebody that actually speaks my language is all the more rare. But that commitment to ruthlessly follow up and follow through until I get you satisfied, that's the thing that's probably the most missing element of all. And yet, it's the critical one for making us feel like I've done the right thing by reaching out.

Walt: Greatly appreciate the sharing today. I greatly appreciate you writing this foreword for us.

David: I call them war stories, but they're not really war stories. They are more like stories from the journey or the road... war stories from the road?

Walt: Absolutely–thanks again!

"The leader's responsibility is to bring their organization and its people from where they are to where they will enjoy future success. They do this by strong relationships with employees, customers, and other key stakeholders, and by guiding the organization to achieve its vision, meet its mission, live its values and fulfil its strategy."

Harry Hertz
Director (retired)
Malcolm Baldrige National Quality Award

Author's Note
(John Vinyard)

David Spong led Boeing Airlift and Tanker in 1998 when they received the Malcolm Baldrige National Quality Award in the Manufacturing Sector. Boeing Airlift and Tanker manufactured the Boeing C-17 military transport.

In 2003 David Spong led Boeing Aerospace Support when they received the Malcolm Baldrige National Quality Award in the Service Sector. Boeing Aerospace Support does not manufacture, but services military aircraft for the Department of Defense.

David was the first leader to receive the Baldrige Award in two different sectors.

It was an honor to work closely with David.

His predecessor had saved the C-17 program from being eliminated by the US Department of Defense. We used to say David's predecessor 'saved the empire,' and then David 'built the roads' by establishing systematic processes for everything, including leadership!

All too often leaders focus on a proud set of Vision, Mission, Values, but forget to focus on the behaviors those drive. It's easy to see groups who had fancy Vision, Mission, Values and in a few minutes, you can tell they have not been translated into behaviors. This is discussed in detail later in the book, and they are presented here for you as well.

Operating Principles

Integrity in all we do–every action, every day

- We tell it like it is

- We will be open and candid in all our dealings

- We respect, honor, and trust one another

- We work toward consensus

- Disagreement is healthy and encouraged, but once a decision is made, we proactively support it

- We have one conversation at a time

- Our silence is consent

- We focus on issues and ideas rather than titles and personalities

- We actively listen and question to understand

- We do not attack the messenger

- We start on time, observe time limits, and structure the agenda to end on time

- We identify clear objectives and expectations for our meetings

- We have a bias for velocity

Have Fun…Enjoy the Journey and Each Other

In addition to David's behavior standards shown here, we have included others in the Appendix. There are three examples which we feel are laudable and give the leader reading this book several views and choices. The Boeing example includes the Behavior Standards used by David and his teams. These behaviors were real, and every time the leadership team met, they spent a few seconds going over them. It was amazing to see those executive leaders change their behavior over time as they embraced these behaviors.

The Malcolm Baldrige National Quality Award

The Malcolm Baldrige National Quality Award® is the highest level of national recognition that a U.S. organization can receive for performance excellence, particularly in relation to resilience and long-term success. The new award criteria for 2024 focus on eight performance dimensions:

- Leadership and Governance

- Strategy

- Operations

- Operational Continuity

- Workforce

- Customers and Markets

- Community Engagement

- Finance

The Baldrige Foundation Board of Directors authorized the E. David Spong Lifetime Achievement Award in 2016.

Recipients must have made a sustained contribution of leadership excellence with exceptional and far-reaching impact on the Baldrige Enterprise in a manner worthy of recognition at the national level.

The committee selects recipients for the Lifetime Achievement Award in recognition of an individual who, like the award's namesake, has performed truly extraordinary service and created a positive and lasting legacy within the quality movement and the Baldrige community. The award recognizes the entirety of the recipient's career, rather than, or in addition to, a single contribution.

Lifetime Achievement Award recipients are credited with changing their world and inspiring others to do the same.

The award is presented each year at the Baldrige Quest for Excellence conference.

Award recipients share how they lead their organizations and inspire their people to achieve high performance and become counselors for excellence throughout the Baldrige community.

SECTION 1

Becoming A Leader

1

What Is a Leader?

Child 1: "I'm in charge."

Child 2: "No. I'm the oldest. I'm in charge."

Child 1: But Dad told me to drive to the store to get milk and eggs, not you. I have my license now, you know?"

Child 2: "Yeah, and I'm going with you because Mom told me to and I'm older, so I'm in charge."

The exchange above, or one very similar, is an often-repeated exchange from most of the families on the planet.

What is a leader? Is it Child 1 who knows the mission and has a charge from Dad? Or is it Child 2, who is older and has a "superior" mission from Mom?

When you are by yourself, you are by default the leader of the mission. It might even be someone else's mission they have assigned to you. But as the person with agency–the ability to act, adjust, or modify–you are the leader.

Child 1 could go to the store by himself or herself. BUT Child 2 is inserted by the mom character, presumably because she perceives risks that may not be seen or anticipated by the younger, less experienced driver.

Notice: The individual child does not need to wrestle with the question, "Am I the leader?" when no one else is involved in the tasking. Only when the second person or more people are added does the question arise.

As soon as there is another person involved in the mission, even children seem to know that someone must be in charge. The person in charge is the leader.

Leadership is always defined in a context of "more than one person engaged in a mission or task."

For most of us, we are born into a family. We have a mother and a father, and we may have siblings. In this context where the children are in training and development mode, and generally the parents are too, the "normal experience" is centered on relative age and experience.

This pattern becomes a truly foundational pattern for us as we exit from the training and development "family" environment to the more demanding and less familiar "work" environment. Do you think that this foundational pattern affects the way you look at the age and experience of your workplace leaders?

For most of us, the answer is obviously a resounding YES. In most of our work environments, the leadership roles default to the more experienced among the teams. This is true up to a certain point, then other factors start to dominate. Factors like capability, competence, vision, communications, empathy, education, experience, etc., become much more important than just the experience factor or "I'm the oldest" frame that our family environments focused on.

Sometimes it's simpler to share a sports framework–the player with the most experience is not always going to be the starter on the sports team. Sometimes the less experienced player has more skills, better fundamentals, more natural talent and can execute better than the player with more time in the position. If you're coaching to win the games, you play the better player, regardless of experience. In business organizations, it's the same.

Who is this book written for?

Drivers. Driving to create value for stakeholders, customers, employees, industries, states, countries, etc., all requires leaders who will steer, accelerate, brake, and adjust as they deem necessary to create that value.

Leaders–this book is written for leaders. We'll unpack what we mean by that word along the way–it is not what most people think. How do we know that...? Here's how: We look at the current state and compare what we find to what we expected to find, and we see a huge gap.

The current state of the world of corporate leadership is awful compared to what we expected. Billions of dollars are spent on "Leadership Training" every year ($370 billion globally and $169 billion in the USA in 2023) and yet, the results and reports are rarely good and--even more rarely--great. According to the Harvard Business Review[1], the time between being appointed to a supervisory or "leadership" position to the time one attends the first training on how to be an effective leader or supervisor is eleven years!

We hear and see so much frustration out there about the "70 percent" failure rate of business transformations, digital transformations, mergers, and major projects. Also, when combined with the frequently reported lack of engagement of employees in companies, there seems to be a need for something to turn this around or at least provide a way for you, the leader or manager at your organization, to avoid getting tossed about in the wake of that massive wave of failure.

We started with an idea that the things we've learned over our combined 90+ years of experience would help anyone in a company or organization that wants to successfully navigate the way to sustainable value creation.

We picked a provocative title. We wanted to reach you somehow, and this is a mechanism for engagement. Welcome to *Driving Behind Idiots*.

---

[1] Harvard Business Review <u>We Wait Too Long to Train Our Leaders</u>

Leadership Isn't as Well Understood as One Might Think

There are exceptionally good companies. There existed within every one of these at one time or another one or more exceptionally effective leaders. There are many, many other companies or other organizations that are not exceptional and are not led by exceptional leaders. In the USA alone, companies spend more than $160 billion every year on leadership training. This is projected to be $260 billion by the year 2030. If you were one of the trainees, what is your take... Was the money well spent? Do you understand what your responsibilities are? Do you understand what the sequence of your steps should be? Maybe even more importantly: Does everybody in your organization have the same approach to leadership and use the same steps?

This DOES NOT mean all leaders have the same skill set, any more than it would be fair to say that all the people with drivers' licenses have the same skill set, or that all football players or ping pong players have the same skill set.

Why start with driving?

When you get behind the wheel of a car YOU ARE THE LEADER OF THAT JOURNEY.

What driver can say they've never experienced being behind another driver that doesn't appear to know the ways of sharing the road? Similarly, what new or seasoned leader or manager hasn't found him or herself reporting to someone who is not meeting expectations associated with "good" or "effective" leadership?

Both of your authors have more than our share of years driving in and around Atlanta, Georgia--the not-so-proud owner of the title for "Worst Driving Experience in the USA," beating out Los Angeles–the previous title holder.

Where are all these drivers coming from and heading to?

Atlanta's roadways are clogged with people traveling to multiple destinations. Friday traffic is particularly heavy due to folks passing through town on the way to or from vacation. But the other drivers sharing the road at rush hour are commuting to work!

Those same commuters, many more than we expect with their poor driving skills, are applying the same logic to their jobs, and making the same kinds of decisions for your company as they do on the roadways.

But we'll talk about more than just driving in this book.

Additionally, Walt grew up in the military (US Air Force) and served on active duty for several years following college. He also spent eight years in high school and college on sports teams (varsity football and many intramural team sports). We'll be bringing some of that background and experience into the discussion of leadership systems. We both strongly believe the gridiron and military environments can provide some additional clarity and perspective to the topics.

To wrap this up and get you behind the wheel, the audience for the book is people like us, who have had the job of driving to get stuff done in organizations.

We will try to help answer the following questions:

- How do you lead when you're not THE leader?

- How do you lead and how do you best follow when the leader that you have doesn't know how to lead?

- How do you feel good about what you're doing in your company, in your role, in an organization where there is no leadership system, and there is no even-handed expectation of what leaders are supposed to do?

As you learned from David Spong in the foreword, to win the Malcolm Baldrige National Quality Award, among the short list of criteria your organization must meet is something called a "leadership system." Following the example of the Deming Prize in Japan and based on Dr. W. Edwards Deming's work in defining Total Quality Management as a key cultural component of the turnaround of the Japanese economy following World War II, the Baldrige Award has become a symbol of organization effectiveness and a point of pride for the employees of companies that have attempted to win, and for those that make it through the journey of assessments and site visits.

Why did the Baldrige Office add a "Leadership System" to the criteria? It already had a robust set of questions describing organizational leadership. From discussion with the Baldrige Director who oversaw the creation of the criteria, Mr. Harry Hertz, he revealed that frequently organizations interpreted "leadership" as only the top few layers of the organization.

Recognizing that leadership was necessary at every level, they required a Leadership System which was used *"throughout the organization."*

Bottom_Line: We believe you will not be able to deploy your leadership style, and the wisdom gained from experience from your senior leadership team, without a systematic approach to leading – a Leadership System.

Ninety-nine percent of 'leadership' books are written about management and not leadership. If they do discuss leadership, they address various components for situations and scenarios and do not tell you what the sequential steps are, or how to make it systematic.

These are the reasons we wrote this book, and we want to share what we've come to understand from leading organizations—both our successes and (sometimes) from doing it the wrong way and learning what not to do next time.

What will you get from this book?

This book will provide access to a leadership navigation toolset. We will present the elements as we go through several discussions using war stories from the road–both real experiences from driving in less-than-ideal conditions and leading change efforts.

We'll introduce some basic ideas–the "blocking and tackling" of leading change, and some less-than-obvious practices that will make you a superstar driver in the race to value.

Core ideas will be explored and mapped as you go through this journey with us–we'll talk about distinctions between consistency, congruence, coherence, and clarity–each one a critical component of your toolset for successfully leading change. As a leader, your followers are constantly looking for predictability from you. All of these "abstract words" like those just mentioned will help you as a leader to show the way to be eminently predictable and a provider of safety and confidence along the change journey.

Do you remember using maps to help get from one location to another? Yes, in the old days, we would reach into a glove box in the car and pull out a printed map. By the way, you can still get these in grocery stores, drug stores, and at state-run welcome centers along the highways. Back then, we would use the information from the date the map was drawn, evaluate possible ways to go, and choose a preferred route. Sometimes, the information on my map was woefully out-of-date, and, on those occasions, trips obviously did not go well or as planned.

Today, we put an address in our phone and usually choose the "fastest route" option, then follow the instructions from the "navigator" to get to the destination. We also see cool features like a shareable estimated time of arrival (ETA). Now, we can tell other interested parties when we'll arrive at the destination–to the minute! These navigation tools tell us about hazards along the route as we go–things like wrecks not yet cleared, lane blockages, debris in the road, and even speed checks from local police or highway patrol units!

How wonderful would it be for your leadership efforts to have that level of predictability and accuracy? We'll show you a way to build that kind of dashboard and score-keeping system for your change effort. We'll help you develop ways of sensing that things are going sideways or outside the lines long before your company car leaves the safety of the smooth roadway.

At the end of the book, you will have a new way of looking at the road ahead, and several new tools to ensure that you can outdrive the other folks sharing your roadways. And, if you're in a competitive "race" in your business or organization, we'll help you get to the finish line and see the checkered flag wave for you, your car, and your team.

Benefits include:

- An ability to train your whole team on a consistent approach to leadership.

- An ability to match each of your actions to a specific point in a Leadership System.

- An ability to do a better job of focusing on what you should spend your time on and eliminating what you should not spend any time on.

- A better ability to measure your progress as you go, and not wait until the end to find out you are not going to be successful.

We've even seen leaders who keep a copy of their leadership system on their desk. If you come in to discuss an issue, they will ask, "Where is this topic on our system?" If it isn't on there, then they should not be wasting time on it.

The Problems of Bad Driving

Though the statistics are hard to find today, we knew even before the fuel crisis of the 1970's, that the drivers who travel fast are not the primary cause of accidents – it's actually (predominantly) the slow, hesitant, distracted drivers who cause most of the issues that clog up the roads. There are many other problematic approaches to driving on our shared roadways that create unnecessary stress or delays.

We'll share how those same traits can be devastating inside your organization, and what to do to navigate successfully when you encounter them. There's usually a way around them, even if you can't avoid them--you typically can't. They are there driving in front of you. "Idiots" may seem like a very harsh word – perhaps the folks you encounter are all genius-level people, but for one reason or another, you'll be frustrated by them because they are one of the following:

- Distracted

- Lost

- Hesitant

- Scared

- Student Drivers

- Ancient Drivers

- Drivers under the influence

- Racers

- Tortoises

- King of the Road–Rude, inconsiderate drivers

- Gracious to a fault, unexpectedly nice drivers

- Backseat Drivers

- Stop at the Yield Sign or roundabout drivers

- Lane Rangers

If you've been driving for a while, you've probably already encountered all of these and maybe a few categories of your own.

Many of the drivers above park in your company's parking lot. You'll encounter them in the hallways and meeting rooms, much the same as when driving on the roadways.

We'll walk you through approaches to each and leave you with strategic as well as tactical means to minimize their impact on your leadership journey.

To mitigate this set of problems, we believe that the correct response is to implement a leadership system. In this book, we will provide you with a systematic process to lead and give you an approach to use--a workbook with a leadership navigation method and supporting tools, which will help you with the pre-work that is the hardest part of successful leadership.

Automobiles come equipped from the factory with rearview mirrors and brakes. The brakes are there to give you confidence to go fast–if you can't slow down or stop, you won't want to go fast! The mirrors are there so you can see what's coming up behind and beside you. These tools are necessary for safe, effective use of the car on shared roadways. Even if there were no other drivers on the roads with you, you would still want these in the car.

"The farther backward you can look,
the farther forward you can see."
Winston Churchill

Just like driving your car from one place to another, leading requires vision. Vision lives in the past, present, and the future. In our cars, we have mirrors on the side and a rearview in the middle so we can see what's behind us and what's coming on the periphery. You will learn to use data from the past to frame the answers to questions about what happened, and data from right now based on what is happening in the present. Most importantly, you and your entire team will be able to see the future and adjust your course around and through the challenges and obstacles on the path.

There are significant differences between driving for commuting/vacation and driving to win in endurance racing:

Driving for Commuting/Vacation:

- The primary goal is transportation from point A to point B safely and efficiently
- Follows all traffic laws and regulations
- Operates the vehicle within normal parameters for fuel efficiency
- Driving is relaxed with frequent breaks as needed
- Little need for high-performance driving dynamics
- Vehicle maintenance is basic for reliable transportation

Driving for Endurance Racing:

- The sole objective is to win the race through speed and skilled performance
- Traffic laws/regulations do not apply on the closed racing circuit
- Vehicles are driven at the absolute limits of their performance capabilities

- Demands intense focus and concentration for hours at a time
- Requires precise car control at extremely high speeds
- Driving technique must account for environmental conditions changing lap to lap
- Success hinges on extracting maximum speed through aggressive racing lines
- Pit stops incorporate radically different driving for entering/exiting pit lane
- Vehicles are meticulously engineered and maintained for peak performance

Key differences come down to priorities, mentality, and operating parameters. Daily driving values safety, efficiency, and legality. Endurance racing demands an uncompromising pursuit of speed, advanced car control skills, and cars finely tuned as racing machines. The driving disciplines are completely distinct in their intended purpose and necessary level of ability.

In your business, are there ways to use the driving metaphor to help you achieve your objectives?

On completion of this book, your toolset will also include items that the average leader will never use–and remember, most of these projects and efforts are failing even though these companies and their leaders are using what are referred to as "best practices."

Best practices are clearly not sufficient for seventy percent or more of change attempts, or for the masses of employees that are currently disengaged at work. Importantly, "best practices" are the result of learning–from past experiences. Novelty and rapid change don't come with best practices or manuals on how to apply them.

Your leadership system is the key tool for dealing with novel situations and rapid change.

Best Practices can be improved, and new practices can be invented, used, and improved to the point where the "new" practice" matures into a "best practice!" Racing (and leadership knowledge and skills) has changed dramatically over the years. Fifty years ago, a good Indianapolis 500 pit stop was 15–18 seconds. Today, the time to change four tires and fill the car with fuel is under 8 seconds. We recently saw a high-performance pit crew complete the entire pit for a formula one car in 1.8 seconds!

If you *don't want to be sitting motionless **in the pit*** while the other drivers are racing down the track, or better still, you really want to win your race, you'll need some more advanced tools that give you and your team the same advantages that a high-performance pit crew gives a winning racer.

Whether you are leading a company, a division, a transformation, a smaller change effort, or continuously improving how your group does things; and whether you are leading a short sprint or an endurance race, you need to be able to adjust your approach based on what the path to victory will look like. And, whether your maintenance upgrade is routine or exceptional, maintenance happens.

It is interesting to note that most commuter driving accidents happen within a few miles of home, when drivers tend to be focused on what's next after the trip since it is nearly over. Most racing accidents happen in the blink of an eye due to errors in judgement, or slower than needed adjustments to suddenly emerging hazards. One size does not fit all.

If you are driving within the neighborhood you live in or making a short trip to the nearby grocery store, you don't spend too much time planning the trip--you just go. On the other hand, if you're going on a two-week vacation at a beach or in the mountains within a one-day drive, you spend quite a bit of time planning because returning for a forgotten item is cost/time prohibitive.

We have a friend who goes camping with his Boy Scout troop every year. He has learned to do a pre-trip trial with the young folks and their families where they pack *as if they're headed to the campsite,* but instead only go to a parking area 30 minutes away to check the gear and equipment.

Why?

Because every year before he implemented this pre-trip ritual, one or more of the campers would get to the campsite and discover he was missing something important. Many of the forgotten items created unnecessary drama and distractions from the intended bonding and learning experience they had planned--like the year the diabetic camper forgot his insulin.

It was the very next year that the Scout Master rolled out his pre-trip check. Bigtime change efforts are no walk in the park, nor are they a scout group's camping trip. You'll need to think through the details to the extent that you can and to the extent that they are known, but what can you do to anticipate the unknowable unknowns and put rituals in place to help your pit crew and team adjust quickly and recover? We have tools for this and will share them with you in this book.

Success Leaves Clues

About thirty percent of leadership efforts, change projects, and transformations get delivered successfully! Think about this--if you agree to oversee one of these efforts it could be career threatening.

What makes it worse for a leader is that surveys show that only approximately thirty-four percent of employees ARE engaged.

What is different about successful teams? Is there anything we can learn about how they added "best practices" to achieve those outcomes?

It turns out that success not only leaves clues, but successful leaders and drivers are usually more than happy to tell others about what they did, how they did it, and what kind of difference it made to deviate from or add to the best practices (just read the interview with David Spong in the Foreword).

Unfortunately, we've also found that many leaders won't ask for the input of others, or worse, if available, they won't take the time to engage in the knowledge sharing offered. We'll share some approaches to properly 'incentivize' your crew to get with and learn from the experienced winners and get that knowledge.

Leadership is not for the weak or the uninformed.

As a leader, you have already seen that while being one of the followers was no piece of cake, leading the followers is more demanding. Knowing about human behaviors and group dynamics is a critical toolset for change leaders. *Force of any kind is met with resistance.* Positive change will be met with positive resistance if you use force to make it happen. Positive change requires many things but the hardest of all is the will to rise above the use of force and to use its opposite to give your car, drivers, and team a chance to win. You must drive forward with heart (Note: Heart is where courage is found).

You must become a teacher.

"First, a leader must be able to teach others in a way that they actually learn. Next, a leader needs to work to discover innovative ways of resolving problems.

How can you train and develop young leaders using Coach John Wooden's recipe for great leadership? (See the breakdown in the appendix).

Source: From Don Yeager's session on LeaderCast 365 in 2023.

Famous Physicist, Richard Feynman's approach to teaching is similar:

He said, "Teach the subject matter to a five-year-old. If they can't learn it from you, you don't understand it well enough to teach it yet." Our followers deserve the same level of teaching capability from their leaders.

A Basic Leadership Perspective

There have been thousands of books written on "leadership," most of which deal with "management," not leadership. In simple terms, they discuss organizational structure, dynamics, inter-working, and many other topics which may help you to understand the organization but may not help you understand what actions you should take as a leader, or in what sequence. Many of the books and many authorities or "thought leaders" on social media speak to the critical need to address "Culture."

BOLD ASSERTION OF TRUTH: Culture is downstream from leadership. Yes, it is true (also) that, "Culture eats strategy for breakfast." Translation: Culture is upstream from strategy. This book on leadership systems gives you the tools needed to lead your culture to a place where it can be a force multiplier instead of a net negative for achieving marketplace objectives.

War Stories from the Road–Culture Priming and Cultural Entropy

During WWII, General Patton took over a war-fighting group and immediately told his officers to always wear the uniform correctly and to make sure that they were always seen as being sharper than the other army members assigned to the location. "Patton's Men" were different. They looked different and they performed at a higher level, too.

Out of high school, I (Walt) was recruited to play on the offensive line of a college football team. Our line coach had created a culture for his group on the team that was distinctly different from any I had ever experienced before (or since). We were "Bubbas."

Many years later, all the young men who played for that coach over the years still gather and talk about how special those experiences and culture were to us as individuals and how the principles have helped us in our lives beyond football. While we were there, we had winning seasons every year and were even nationally ranked one year.

While in the US Air Force's Officer Training School in San Antonio, I (Walt) was fortunate to be assigned to Squadron 9 under the leadership of a regular USAF Captain (and fighter pilot). I was welcomed to the squadron by the upperclassmen and taken to an assembly of all the new trainees, where we would meet our new leader. The upperclassmen let us know that we were fortunate to be assigned to this squadron and that we were a different breed from the rest of the trainees. We were part of the

Red-Hot Squadron and, "We win everything." We were instructed to raise the roof with applause and chants when Capt. Cooley was introduced. This did not happen for the other Squadron Commanders in squadrons one through eight, but when Capt. Cooley was announced, we raucously applauded and chanted as instructed.

Long story greatly shortened—over the next few months we won everything, all the individual and group awards went to our squadron. Our culture had been primed for success.

Any system or organization will decay over time without maintenance—your culture is also a system that can fall to cultural entropy. The answer to a decayed or decaying culture is the implementation of an effective leadership system.

Congratulations on having the humility to pick up and read this book.

The best leaders we have known have humility, understand what is important, and in what order things need to be done.

That's what this book is intended to do. Our goal is to:

1. Give leaders a perspective of the team they are leading.

2. Give leaders a systematic way to lead:

   a. What's most important
   b. What to start with
   c. The sequence of steps

d. What NO LEADER CAN DELEGATE

Leaders must understand the difference between knowledge and wisdom. Years ago, a Japanese professor who was on the Deming Award Committee (one of Japan's most coveted awards) told us the following: "Knowledge can be taught, but wisdom must be observed."

Because of his insight, we have included "Winner's Circles" throughout this book so you can benefit from the wisdom we have observed over the years.

Reflecting on years of leading (some good, some bad), this insight rings true. Some of the most memorable teaching moments were when a leader showed wisdom in a perspective or direction.

Leadership has hundreds of definitions, and we certainly won't try to set a new standard in a definition. For this book a leader is a person who is leading at least one other person.

Leadership is not necessary or common in every action a manager takes. The context establishes the need to lead. A US Army saying summarizes the importance of leadership: "No one ever 'managed' anyone into battle."

The leader does not have to be the biggest, best, smartest, or fastest, but the leader does need to be viewed as doing more for the team than adding just one more vote.

Hundreds of schools teach what they advertise as "leadership." In this book we will present a systematic way to lead.

Leadership becomes more complex as the work environment becomes more complex. And the work environments do become much more complex than the simple "family" context, or the team sports context. The tasks and missions involve much more than the relatively simple chores of one's youth.

An important concept of leadership is "When the leader gives someone the assignment and/or authority to lead something (i.e., a group or project), it is instantly disempowering for the leader to step in and second-guess or contradict the person they just assigned. Most of us have experienced this during our careers. In simple terms, "If you give me an assignment, let me do it." It is important to note, however, if the leader sees the person is about to make a critical mistake, the senior leader may be required to step in.

If this really is required:

- Do it in a way that does not undercut the authority of the person you just assigned to lead the project.

- Typically, you will want to do this in private.

- Do it in a timely manner–don't tell them what they did wrong 'yesterday.' That is too late for them to make a course correction.

- Do it in a manner where they understand the "why" of your urgency.

*"A leader must have humility and
a passionate drive for results."*
Paul Worstell
President
ProTec Coating
Malcolm Baldrige National
Quality Award Recipient

A theory for you to consider: The Military Leadership System is more mature than almost any other.

As the risks increase in the mission, the necessity for leadership increases. In the military, where lives are on the line, you will find a particularly rigorous centering or focus on the importance of effective leadership and leaders at every level of the organization.

The risks of warfare and battle require this focus. The military context, as compared to most business contexts, demands a higher commitment—that of potentially losing one's life in pursuit of the organization's objectives. Most businesses do not require this level of commitment. Surprisingly, despite the obvious maturity of the military's leadership approach, very few of the corporate and business organizations look there for guidance in how they lead.

However, there have been a few:

- Ross Perot's experience at IBM and his background and appreciation of the military approach saw him adopt some of those strategies at EDS and later at Perot Systems.

- In the book, *Good to Great*, Jim Collins studied thirteen companies that had outperformed others in a niche of the marketplace. He found that each of them had in common an approach to leadership and a system of working together that resonates on the same pattern or frequency as the military leadership system or a Baldrige Award leadership system.

- In contrast, many of the companies highlighted in the Tom Peters book, *In Search of Excellence*, did not have a consistent pattern and many of them, while excellent for a brief time, did not sustain excellence in operational performance and many did not survive the changing realities of the marketplace–even household names like Kodak, DEC, and K-Mart.

In the United States, we have had for several years a national awards program to recognize companies and non-government organizations (NGOs) for **operational excellence**. Built on the model of Japan's Deming Prize, our Baldrige Award (The Malcolm Baldrige National Quality Award, administered by the US Department of Commerce) recognizes companies for sustained operational excellence, and has very specific criteria and assessment processes for nominees. In this book, we are focused on the criteria that require implementation and successful usage of a leadership system.

Leadership is defined by the context or backdrop--not just the situation. In any group of people working together, when a situation arises that calls for leadership, the context for that situation will exert enormous influence over how the leader emerges. For example, in a hierarchical organization, people will look for the designated leader first.

In a self-organizing group, the situation itself may dictate the leader based on experience or familiarity, in which case the team will defer to whomever is the most familiar or experienced to guide the team's response and path forward from the event or situation. In some senses, this is a pattern recognition game–and even in the traditional, top-down, hierarchy, the designated leader is assumed to have the background and training to respond as a leader as the situation presents itself, and as it changes. He or she is assigned the role of leader.

What happens when this approach fails, and the designated leader does not have a clear vision and a competent reaction? Our answer to this question is:

- Seventy percent or higher opportunity for failure:

    o Seventy percent of change initiatives fail according to frequently cited papers from McKinsey and Bain – both consulting companies looking for business.
    o Approximately 70 percent of most company's employees are disengaged according to Gallup (Jan 24, 2024 – 76 percent of employees).

Doing the thumbnail math then, for most organizations there is a thirty percent success rate at making necessary changes to survive and thrive in an increasingly dynamic marketplace.

Seventy percent fail. Thirty percent succeed. Or at least that's what we're led to believe.

David Wilkinson, Editor-in-Chief of the Oxford Review, investigated to evaluate the truth of these percentages and found them severely wanting in substantiation. According to his research[2] the seventy percent failure assertion is not supported with any meaningful proof. However, there is a large acceptance of the assertion in the marketplace and in social media. Why is this so easily accepted as gospel when it is not substantiated with evidence? I (Walt) suspect that we believe this because we know from our own personal experience that getting individuals and groups to change is often very challenging. So, seventy percent failure and thirty percent success at attempted change via implementations of software, new tools and technologies in other areas, or new business models, processes and procedures are not unbelievable – they are all too believable. And, importantly, these are not the kind of odds that make one want to take on the charge.

However, some do succeed and if you follow David Wilkinson's research-supported view it is greater than thirty percent of the attempts that do so. Our suggestion is that you and your leadership team take the bull by the horns and follow the model of those that

---

[2] https://youtu.be/_xle0yoKYKM?si=ZfLnvTXGUW2YDptZ

succeed -- by designing and implementing your own leadership system and implementing behaviors which will drive success.

With a leadership system, you have a framework for each designated leader to know what he or she is responsible for accomplishing and how they will be held accountable and rewarded for getting that body of work done. Without that core understanding, people will be very busy doing things but may not be accomplishing much with regards to mission and purpose. And, when the hierarchy is not capable of leading, the leadership system will be there to support a non-hierarchical leader to find and fill the gaps to get the job done.

We'll unpack for you how to design and implement a leadership system for your company (see the *Appendix: Developing Your Leadership System* where we describe how you can develop your own) and, how to ensure that it is uniquely your company's leadership system with high engagement and ownership up, down, and sideways in your organization.

Your company has its own culture. Your culture could be a strength, or it can be a profound anchor holding you back. Note the adage referenced in the first War Story from the Road– "Culture eats Strategy for breakfast." Culture is defined by your leadership system. We'll cover this in great depth as it is clearly critical to organizational performance and to survival.

War Stories from the Road -- Freedom vs. Control

In several conversations the tensions between freedom and control along with the tensions between safety and chaos/anarchy were central and thought-provoking elements. Over the years I (John) have spent driving in the United States and Canada, and as a passenger in England, Spain, and India, these tensions are ever present. In most circumstances, as a driver you have freedom, but your freedom is bounded or constrained by statutes—most obviously things like speed limits, stop signs and traffic lights, but less obviously by the norms of driving on the right and passing on the left, yielding to faster travelers, and the expectations of order at a four-way stop intersection.

At a more abstract level, these tensions define many of the problems of leadership. How much freedom and autonomy do you provide to your followers? How much control is too much or too little? Is your workplace safe enough to provide the freedom to be authentic, or is it unsafe to the point that your workers feel pressured to conform rather than stand out?

As a passenger in India on my first trip to the country, I was surprised to see the variety of vehicles and animals sharing the roadways. It was a tremendous mix of high-end cars and trucks driving with individuals and families on scooters, motorized bicycles, and carts or wagons. Lots of pedestrians in the cities along with dogs and cows were also sharing the roads. None of them seemed to pay attention to the lines on the roads that defined the lanes. The ability to gain entrance to a flow of traffic is severely constrained by the volume of participants, and one has to be willing to take some risk in entering a moving flow of traffic.

In Bangalore (India's "Silicon Valley"), I (Walt) got into a vigorous discussion about using Artificial Intelligence (AI) to better manage the flows of traffic in general, but the expert and I agreed that an AI solution in India would be far more challenging to build and execute than one in Atlanta. The number of variables is one factor, and the number of possible control points is another. In India the variable number is significantly higher, and the number of traffic controls is significantly lower. Also, in India the "hard and fast" rules of the road we assume in the USA are less hard and fast.

Nevertheless, Bangalore pulled off something that most would say is impossible. On one weekend they changed all the roads from two-way to be forevermore "one-way." As an American I view this as one of the most amazing achievements ever.

Whether in Bangalore or Atlanta, the ultimate challenge to the introduction and adoption of managed traffic is one of moving drivers away from autonomy and toward a more controlled method of travel. The more we introduce a controlled or modulated travel experience whether thru "Smart City" technologies to regulate the flow of autonomous drivers such as variable speed limits based on volume, or managed timing of traffic lights, we are ultimately increasing the controls and limiting the autonomy or freedom of the driver. When we go all the way to autonomous vehicles, where presumably the human driver is not in charge or in control of the vehicle, and the machine or algorithm is driving, the car's AI brain is selecting the best route and managing change without input or interference from a human driver, or, should we say, occupant or passenger?

Over the many years of living and driving in Atlanta, I've seen the policy makers express a desire to reduce the number of vehicles on the roadways. They use marketing to push commuters toward the use of carpools and offer a benefit to them by creation of High Occupancy Vehicle (HOV) lanes. HOV lanes are not broadly used, and the concept continues to fail.

Why? Because the carpool is a constraint on the freedom of each of the members, who must give up autonomy to get the benefit of driving past the other participants on the road during rush hours. For most drivers, giving up the freedom of going when they want and where they want without having to get agreement from the other members of the pool is a price too high to pay to get the relatively minor benefit of fewer minutes in traffic.

I've also seen the push to use Mass Transit, like our Metro Atlanta Regional Traffic Authority trains and buses, fail over and over for the same reasons. Having to find a route from a bus to a train with frequent stops and changes is not enough of a time-saver or stress-reliever for the benefit of not having to drive in traffic. And again, you lose the freedom to come and go as you please, because you are at the mercy of the train and bus schedules (and reliability). Because the ask is counter to individual autonomy and the benefit is weak by comparison, these pushes are doomed to continued failure. And the traffic continues to grow as the city grows.

How does this relate to Leadership in organizations?

A pendulum swings continuously in organizations between the drive for centralization and standards-driven performance versus decentralization and local autonomy to define how work gets done, and, critically important to the life of the organization, *how value gets created*. There are pros and cons for both extremes. Clearly, the drive for centralization is focused on a desire for efficiency of operations – lower costs to produce higher volumes of goods or services.

The drive for decentralization prioritizes a desire to have more creativity or sensitivity to local market conditions to deliver differentiated goods or services that the market desires. One can easily see that each offers high value but both approaches are context specific. Mass production is not the same as unique or custom production.

Mass production practices do not fit well in artisan marketplaces. Nor do "artisan" food items work well in cafeteria settings–they are better suited to fine restaurants. As you explore your business context, you will see many opportunities to choose a pattern that best fits your people and their marketplaces.

Context is Critical

Is this a "mass production" business where we don't need much - if any - creativity or imagination? If we just need workers to keep the line moving, should we find or build machines for this? Humans thrive on creativity and imagination outlets -- and shrivel when there are no channels for differentiated (personal) service.

Is this a place where each customer is looking for a unique product or service? If so, we will need very talented staff members to listen to and understand those market needs and respond. The opportunity to achieve efficiency will be dramatically lower and will come in the form of back-office standardization versus customer-facing cookie-cutters. And though each product or service is specific to the client, you can define a standard for customer experience that drives repeat purchases. You will have to look for places to find efficiencies.

Is this a hybrid company with a combination of mass-produced items and differentiated, unique offerings? If so, how will you decide to automate where you can and remain creative where you can't? How will you hire and staff these positions? How will you keep humans engaged? These are not always simple questions, which often means looking outside for opinions from others to help us decide how to lead our people in our business in our markets.

Looking Outside: Great Thinkers Thinking About Leadership

People who study leaders and leadership have come to some profound insights. Here are a couple of our favorites and a summary for each:

Dave Snowden is a thought leader in the field of organizational leadership and complexity science. Some of his key insights on leadership include:

1. Emphasizing the importance of context: Snowden argues that leaders must understand the specific context in which they operate to be effective.

2. Advocating for a cyclical, non-linear approach to decision-making: Snowden suggests that leaders should adopt a more flexible, cyclical approach to decision-making, as opposed to a linear, cause-and-effect approach.

3. Focusing on sense-making, not decision-making: Snowden believes that the role of leaders is to help their organizations make sense of their environment, rather than simply make decisions.

4. Promoting decentralized decision-making: Snowden advocates for a more decentralized approach to leadership, where decisions are made at the lowest possible level, rather than being centralized at the top.

5. Emphasizing the importance of storytelling: Snowden argues that leaders should use storytelling to engage their organizations and build a shared understanding of the organization's context, goals, and values.

I (Walt) have found Snowden's body of work enormously helpful as a change leader–one can't know or see everything going on and leadership, by definition, is a team sport. Snowden's Cynefin Framework is particularly useful for setting expectations at the beginning of a huge change and for getting effective governance in place for deciding as the effort progresses when the inevitable unknowable unknowns show up.

The Leadership Challenge by **James M. Kouzes** and **Barry Z. Posner** is a popular book on leadership that outlines five practices for effective leadership. The key points from the book are:

1. Model the Way: Leaders must demonstrate their values and beliefs through their actions and decisions, setting an example for others to follow.

2. Inspire a Shared Vision: Leaders must articulate a compelling vision for the future and inspire others to work towards it.

3. Challenge the Process: Leaders must encourage others to continuously improve and seek new and innovative ways of doing things.

4. Enable Others to Act: Leaders must empower others and provide them with the resources and support they need to be successful.

5. Encourage the Heart: Leaders must recognize and celebrate the accomplishments of their followers, creating a positive and inspiring work environment.

These five practices are presented as a framework for developing leadership skills, and the authors emphasize that leadership is a continuous process of learning and growth. *The Leadership Challenge* is widely regarded as a seminal work in the field of leadership, and its principles have been applied in a variety of settings, including business, non-profit organizations, and government.

I (Walt) wrote some of my master's thesis on leadership development using material from an early version of *The Leadership Challenge*. The authors' focus on the heart resonates very much in alignment with my experiences from team sports in high school and college and well as our focus on "esprit de corps" in the military. Leadership is not precise or cold and logical. We're leading people, not machines.

Over the years, we've also looked back in time to gain insights from some of the great leaders in history. Here are a few examples:

Great Leader Examples and Contrasts

Alexander the Great was a military leader and king of Macedonia who conquered much of the known world and laid the foundation for the Hellenistic Age. His leadership strategies were characterized by a combination of personal charisma, military tactics, and an unwavering pursuit of his goals. Some of the key leadership strategies that he employed include:

1. Visionary thinking: Alexander had a clear vision of what he wanted to achieve, and he communicated this vision to his army, inspiring them to follow him into battle.

2. Flexibility: He was flexible in his approach and was willing to adapt his strategies to changing circumstances, making quick and effective decisions.

3. Use of propaganda: Alexander used propaganda and storytelling to create a sense of unity and purpose among his troops, and to build a positive image of himself as a leader.

4. Military tactics: He was a skilled military commander who employed innovative tactics to defeat larger armies. He also placed a strong emphasis on training and discipline, ensuring that his troops were well prepared for battle.

5. Cultural integration: Alexander was a firm believer in cultural integration and encouraged his soldiers to adopt local customs and traditions, fostering a sense of unity and respect among diverse cultures.

Overall, Alexander's leadership strategies were characterized by his ability to inspire and lead his army, his strategic vision, and his willingness to adapt and overcome obstacles.

Much of what we know and define as the military leadership system is directly derived from Alexander the Great. His systems for leading, inspiring, communicating, and staff development have been copied for years. Frederick the Great from Prussia was a great admirer of Alexander, and his studies resulted in the Prussian Military School and much of that set of military philosophy is still very much alive in our US Military Leadership System.

For example, a great admirer of Frederick the Great was our US Army General "Blackjack" Pershing. Pershing (after whom the tanks are named), had a Lieutenant with him in Mexico named George Patton, Jr. Years later, having risen through the ranks, **General George Patton, Jr.** was an American military leader who played a key role in the Allied victory in World War II. His leadership style was marked by his outspoken personality, aggressive tactics, and strict discipline. Some of the key leadership strategies that he employed include:

1. Confidence and determination: Patton was known for his unwavering confidence and determination, which inspired his troops to follow him into battle. He also projected an image of strength and courage, which earned him the respect of his soldiers.

2. Attention to detail: Patton was meticulous in his planning and preparation, ensuring that his troops were well equipped and well trained for battle. He placed a strong emphasis on discipline and attention to detail, which helped to ensure the success of his military operations.

3. Aggressive tactics: Patton was known for his aggressive tactics, which often resulted in rapid victories. He was not afraid to take risks and was willing to use unconventional methods to achieve his goals.

4. Inspiring speeches: Patton was famous for his motivational speeches, which he used to inspire his troops and boost their morale. Patton's communication style was intentionally gritty, and he used a great deal of profane language to make his point with his soldiers. He believed that a positive mental attitude was just as important as physical strength and preparation.

5. Understanding of soldiers: Patton had a deep understanding of soldiers and their needs, and he made a point of visiting his troops regularly and building strong personal relationships with them. He also recognized the importance of taking care of his soldiers and ensuring their well-being.

Overall, General George Patton's leadership style was marked by his confidence, determination, attention to detail, aggressive tactics, and ability to inspire his troops. He was widely regarded as one of the most effective military leaders of his time, and his legacy continues to influence modern military leadership.

General George Washington was the first President of the United States and one of the most important leaders in American history. He was known for his integrity, determination, and strategic thinking, and his leadership strategies played a key role in the success of the American Revolution and the eventual formation of the United States. Some of the key leadership strategies employed by General Washington include:

1. Integrity: Washington was known for his strong moral character and unwavering integrity, which earned him the respect of his soldiers and the American people. He set a high standard for ethical behavior and held himself accountable to his principles.

2. Strategic thinking: Washington was a skilled strategist who was able to think ahead and plan for the long term. He was able to balance his military objectives with his political goals, and he was often able to find creative solutions to complex problems.

3. Adaptability: Washington was flexible and adaptable in his approach, and he was willing to change his strategies as circumstances dictated. He was able to adjust his tactics to meet the changing needs of the war, and he was quick to capitalize on opportunities as they arose.

4. Leadership by example: Washington was known for leading by example, and he often put himself in harm's way to demonstrate his commitment to the cause. He demonstrated bravery and courage on the battlefield, and he inspired his troops to follow his lead.

5. Empowerment of subordinates: Washington believed in empowering his subordinates and delegating authority. He trusted his generals and allowed them to exercise their own judgment in battle, which allowed for more efficient and effective operations.

Overall, General George Washington's leadership strategies were characterized by his integrity, strategic thinking, adaptability, leadership by example, and empowerment of subordinates. He remains one of the most revered leaders in American history, and his legacy continues to inspire generations of leaders.

Contrasts: As you can see from the examples above of three widely acknowledged "Great Leaders," it might be very difficult for you to borrow the style of any one of them for yourself or to pull together all the attributes without understanding the substance behind the styles. For example, George Washington would never adopt George Patton's communication style. The two leadership styles conflicted. This realization almost always results in a discussion as follows in the next section. Alexander the Great's flamboyant style of out-front leadership also contrasts with George Washington's more reserved, but still out-front style. This highlights the need for you to seek your own personal leadership style that is authentic to who you are, not someone else. Like leadership itself, this can be developed over time.

Are Leaders Born or Developed?

Many leaders find themselves in a leadership position suddenly without much preparation or training. There are studies that show many individuals are promoted into a management job years before they attend the first leadership training event sponsored by the company.

To make it worse, as previously stated, most "leadership" training is not really training in leadership, but training in management.

Contrast that with the leadership crucible of the US military, where from the very outset, individuals are actively being trained and prepared for leadership, and this is nearly continuous throughout their time in the military.

Planning & Leadership Model

VALUES

VISION

METRICS

STRATEGIES

PROJECTS

TASKS

Planning Model

A project is a definable delegatable achievement and the key to entrepreneurial rather than bureaucratic behavior.

All communication occurs in the mind of the listener

Listen > Learn > Help > Lead

Appreciative understanding
(active listening between the sentences)
TRUE PRAGMATISM
(Listen for new facts and perceptions)
Leadership Model

In the military system, we believe that every soldier, airman, seaman, and marine will be a leader at some point in the future and rather than wait until after that point to train and prepare, we train and prepare long before the point when leadership skills are required. For many of us who have served in the military, it is quite a shock to see this "horse-cart" inversion in the non-military organizations.

The Planning and Leadership model above is from the US Army Doctrine and Training Command and was in use from 1979-1984. The biggest key here is in the task level bar that says Listen > Learn > Help > Lead.

If you jump out of your lane into someone else's area of expertise, you might want to use this method to engage. Don't start by asserting your leadership, instead start by listening and learning and even by helping in the process they are engaged in—once they know you have listened, learned, and applied that knowledge by helping, you will be way ahead in your ability to lead from your domain of expertise to solve problems for them in their domain. The US Army knew this and wrote it all down in the 70's.

For example, the U.S. Military uses several frameworks for leadership and planning, but one of the core models is the Strategic Leadership Primer developed by the U.S. Army War College:

The Strategic Leadership Primer outlines three primary roles of strategic leaders:

1) Leadership Skills

- Leading organizations and motivating people
- Building and guiding teams
- Making decisions under pressure
- Communicating vision and direction

2) Operating Skills

- Strategic planning and execution
- Resource management
- Assessing strategic environment
- Transitioning between offense/defense

3) Conceptual Skills

- Systems understanding
- Strategic thinking and vision
- Dealing with ambiguity
- Ethical reasoning

It emphasizes key competencies like agility, expertise, intelligence, interpersonal tact, conviction, and courage.

For planning, the U.S. Military uses variants of the Operations Process Model:

1. Planning - Mission analysis, course of action development

2. Preparation - Revisiting the plan, rehearsals

3. Execution - Implementation and adjustment

4. Assessment - Monitoring progress towards objectives

This cyclical model emphasizes the need for continuous assessment and revision based on unfolding conditions during execution.

Other core tenets include the Principles of Joint Operations like objective, offensive, mass, economy of force, maneuver, unity of command, security, surprise, and simplicity.

The military leadership models stress attributes like integrity, expertise, critical thinking, decisiveness and leading by example - while planning highlights meticulous preparation yet flexibility to adapt to changing circumstances.

In the military, despite the many misperceptions about military culture from movies and television, what is real for us on active duty and in the memories we share as veterans is this: We have a very mature leadership system that is intentionally designed to create leaders at every level of the organization wherein any one of the members may be called upon to exercise leadership at some point. Our communications system is designed to move from the commander's intent to a written order carried or transmitted to the leaders in the field and is designed to minimize confusion and chaos in an environment (war or battle) that has chaos built into it from the get-go. Our culture is designed intentionally to build "esprit de corps" or "bands of brothers." Teamwork is essential for warfighting. Teamwork and planning are essential to winning--whether lives are on the line or not.

Are there natural-born leaders? [John] Yes, but *most of us are not natural-born leaders.*

We have all seen natural-born leaders. The things they do out of their gut are all the right things. Natural-born leaders are few and far-between. Most of us must really work at being a leader.

One of the shortcomings we've seen in some natural-born leaders is that they do not always realize that the rest of us do not have the same ability. What is obvious to natural-born leaders requires hard work on the part of most other leaders.

> *"My father always asked, "Are you trying to do something, or be somebody?" Those answers will drive different actions."*
> **Ken Davis**
> **Chief Medical Officer (Retired)**
> **Christus San Antonio**

All of us remember some of our first leadership experiences. One of mine (John) was shuttling between leading two projects–one in Dhahran, Saudi Arabia and the other in San Francisco. I did poorly at leading both. Given the travel, I could only be at each of them a small amount of the time. If I had that choice today, I would decline that stretch. If I had to lead the two, I would do a lot better at defining all the expectations "when I returned." I shudder to think of what my defining moments were on both of those projects.

The following table can help us get a global view of natural-born leaders vs. the rest of us. I remember coaching a natural-born leader named Charlie. One of the things we taught Charlie to do was to observe (i.e., in a meeting) when others "got it," when the point they were discussing was so obvious to him. This was extremely helpful to him understanding that everybody was not at his level of leadership.

Think about which quadrant you fall into, and in which quadrant the other leaders you work with are. Sorry, the bad news is that we are not always the best judge of our leadership skills. In this regard, and in some of the exercises later in the book, gaining the perspectives of others can be enlightening and very helpful. It does, however, require you to swallow enough pride to listen, evaluate, and ACT.

Leadership Traits		Natural Born Leader	
		Yes (Very Few)	No (Most of Us)
Works At Leadership	Yes	Great Leader	Can Be a Great Leader Through a Lot of Work
	No	Good Leader	Should Not Lead

It is humbling to realize most of us are in the right-hand column. Just like "kids did not come with instructions for parents" when most of us became a leader "it did not come with instructions," AND we weren't born knowing what to do.

It may be a humbling exercise but ask a dozen people who know you to list the top five natural-born leaders they have ever observed. Are you on the list? Then ask them to put you in one of the boxes anonymously. Although painful to see, it may open your senses to a path to improve, or at a minimum a path to understand the impressions you make on those around you.

"Heartset" vs. Mindset

We could write for days about the importance of being a "good" leader. We can write many volumes on the havoc created by "bad" leaders. It can be quite therapeutic to write all of that about real people who have lived life as a leader and found themselves in the wrong group at the end of the road.

In chapter 9 of the book, we'll talk about creating a virtual mentors group. For now, let me (Walt) share that virtual mentors are men and women who have departed this life and moved on to the next level of the game. However, they left behind written works or videos in a few cases that lets me "ask" them, "Based on your life's values and principles, what would you advise me to do now in my current situation, to make things better?"

Our mentor group includes people that you would know, like Teddy Roosevelt and George Patton, and many people that you wouldn't know, like Col Robert Wade and Col John Politi, two men I served under in the US Air Force.

Each member of my mentor group had a particular mindset about the role and function of a leader. More importantly, each of them had what I call a particular "heartset" about it as well.

We believe that the "heartset" is more relevant and important than the mindset. Here's why: The rational or logical mind can only take you to the edges of the mental box.

The people you are leading are multidimensional – there is always an emotional and a spiritual basis to understanding each one of them. Therefore, as a leader, you also must have that same multidimensional frame to guide you past the logical edges and into the ethos, culture, vision, values, and to be able to care for your people's "multidimensional boxes."

Many of the most widely read authors on leadership share this understanding. Here are some examples:

Kouzes and Posner (previously referenced) are leadership experts who have studied and written extensively on the behaviors and practices of exemplary leaders. Their book *The Leadership Challenge* is one of the most influential works on leadership.

The Five Practices of Exemplary Leadership:

Their core framework identifies five key practices that successful leaders demonstrate:

- Model the Way-Clarify values and lead by example
- Inspire a Shared Vision-Envision future possibilities and enlist others
- Challenge the Process-Search for opportunities and take risks
- Enable Others to Act-Foster collaboration and build trust
- Encourage the Heart-Recognize contributions and celebrate victories

Some of their key ideas and quotes:

"The truth is that credibility is the foundation of leadership." - They emphasize leaders must be believable and worthy of trust.

"Leaders aren't Born, they're made" - Leadership can be learned through deliberate practice of skills and processes.

"The best leaders are able to bring into focus whatever must confront us. They then rally colleagues to pursue the vision."

"Before you can embrace the new, you have to let go of the past." - On challenging the status quo.

"Leaders make it possible for others to do good work." - Enabling and empowering others is critical.

Their evidence-based findings emphasize that leadership is an observable set of skills and abilities that are learnable, making leaders through dedicated application of key practices and behaviors. Their work provides practical guidance for developing oneself as an effective leader.

Warren Bennis (1925-2014) was a pioneering scholar in the field of leadership studies. His seminal book *On Becoming a Leader* published in 1989 helped shape modern thinking around effective leadership.

Some of his key ideas and quotes include:

The Crucibles of Leadership

- Bennis believed true leaders emerge by having their characters and mettle tested by crucible experiences - intense, transformational periods that force people to question themselves. He said, "It's the crucibles of our lives that create leaders."

Leaders vs Managers

- He drew a sharp distinction between leaders, who influence and inspire, versus managers who simply maintain the status quo. "Managers do things right, leaders do the right thing."

Emotional Intelligence

- Bennis emphasized how great leaders have high emotional intelligence - self-awareness, self-management, social awareness, and relationship skills. "A leader never lies to himself, especially about himself."

Learning Agility

- He stressed leaders must have insatiable learner mindsets to continually grow. "Leaders are people who are willing to change when change becomes essential for survival."

Empowerment

- Bennis advocated for leaders to empower and build credibility with followers through trust and integrity. "Leaders make things possible—they release potential."

Other notable quotes:

"The manager accepts the status quo; the leader challenges it."

"Leaders keep their eyes on the horizon, not just the bottom line."

"Failing leaders embrace process, outstanding leaders focus on results."

Bennis' work highlighted how leadership flows from character, integrity and emotional wisdom over just hierarchical authority or skills. His human-centric ideas continue shaping leadership development today.

When I l(Walt) look back, the "good" leaders in my career all had this heartset that preceded the mindset, and they all had the best interests of the people and the company at heart prior to deciding anything. The "bad" leaders let their own ego or self-centered notions guide them to decisions that were ultimately harmful to the companies and to the people.

There are no perfect people. And there are no perfect leaders who always get it right. But as a follower, we can easily forgive and give grace to someone whose heart was in the right place but got the logic or the underlying assumptions wrong. It is, however, amazingly difficult to forgive or give grace to someone who makes a bad choice for the wrong reasons or knowingly at the expense of others.

Having just recently observed that experience at a twenty-plus year-old company that went out of business due to a misguided heartset, we can tell you that this hurts the employees and key partners far more than just a market shift that went bad.

When the company's competition essentially got it right--in that same shifting marketplace--but this company leader refused to acknowledge the reality of the marketplace, and more importantly refused to listen to the evidence provided by his leadership team--those flawed decisions are hard to put behind you. I can imagine that the people at Enron felt much the same regarding their boss and the other leaders that helped build that house of cards and profited handsomely along the way. If you're not familiar with the Enron story, please see the book by Bethany McLean and Peter Elkin, *The Smartest Guys in the Room*. In the write up on Amazon it describes the story this way: "It is a story of greed, arrogance, and deceit—a microcosm of all that can go wrong with American business."

The ethos of a leader and the ethical framework that flows from that ethos turns out to be the most critical element of a culture. Whatever the leader tolerates grows and expands. If the leader allows bullies and cowards to exist and thrive, the culture responds by producing more bullies and cowards. If the leader tolerates rudeness, you get a proliferation of rude people in your company. After a while, all that's left is the wrong stuff and all the competent, capable people will depart. They will leave you on the island with those who can't go anywhere else.

On the other hand, when you have a leader that nips those behaviors in the bud so they never flower in the organization, the result is a culture of safety and increasing authenticity – where individuals can be liberated to bring more of their strengths and capabilities to the team, and one in which the weaknesses are acknowledged and are openly regarded as part of the skills matrix that will be considered when working together or delegating tasks. Openness and transparency are typically valued highly for this reason. Keeping secrets is seen as a form of manipulation or power-mongering.

Another way of looking at this heartset topic is to focus on the contrast between leaders who seek to have control versus leaders who seek to challenge and get the best from their teams. Openness leads to liberty or autonomy. Closedness leads to anxiety and fear.

How do you make sure you hire for the open heartset versus the control or closed heartset?

Hire slowly and fire fast

When you have a group of senior leaders in a room ask, "Has anybody made a mistake in who they hired?" Our experience is the entire room flinches—because most of us have made that mistake.

A CEO recently told us, "The person I interviewed, and the person who showed up for the job, were not the same person."

TRUETT CATHY, FOUNDER OF THE CHICK-FIL-A FRANCHISES, TOLD A GREAT STORY ONE EVENING. HE WAS AT THE ATLANTA HISTORY MUSEUM TO RECEIVE AN AWARD, AND PRIOR TO THE CEREMONY, AS OTHER GUESTS WERE ARRIVING, TRUETT WAS SHARING WITH A SMALL GROUP OF BUSINESS LEADERS THAT HE HAD JUST RETURNED FROM WASHINGTON, DC, WHERE HE HAD SPOKEN TO A JOINT SESSION OF THE HOUSE AND SENATE ON THE TOPIC OF BUSINESS ETHICS.

HE SAID, "DO YOU KNOW WHAT I TOLD 'EM? I TOLD 'EM THERE WAS NO SUCH THING AS A BUSINESS WITH ETHICS — A BUSINESS HIRES PEOPLE AND THOSE PEOPLE HAVE ETHICS AND USE THEM, OR THEY HAVE NONE AND DON'T."

AS A BUSINESS LEADER YOU PAY THE PRICE FOR THE TIMES WHEN THEY DON'T.

Take your time to evaluate the candidates for how they treat people in positions lower than theirs, and how they treat people with no power.

Many of the bad hires interviewed well. They know how to answer the screening questions and make a positive impression. Many of them present very favorable images. But take your time. Take them out to eat. See how they treat others. Understand where they came from and how they acted there.

Do not only ask for "who liked the person," but listen to the detractors. Years ago, I (John) hired a person into a key position. We sent him to several of our factories. Essentially everyone liked him except one person. After hiring him I realized the one person was exactly right! I didn't listen because everybody else liked him.

Many candidates can make it through the hiring process, and you later find out they are not who they represented. Eliminate them quickly. In my experience, I've personally never been able to coach these folks, and I've never seen anyone else who could either.

You might call this a "misrepresentation." You might also call it, more directly, a lie. Who they say they are is not who they really are. And, whether they are lying to you, to themselves, or to others in your company doesn't matter much—what matters is the disconnect between who you need in the position and who they really are when you're not around.

Hiring slowly and firing fast is the right answer for making sure your business has ethical individuals in decision-making roles. Another solid approach is to implement a leadership system that defines these expectations and clarifies the behaviors desired, and the accountability needed to stay in a leadership role within your company. Another way to improve your odds and reduce your risks is to hire everyone as a contractor for 90 days. At the end of the period, the bad fits will be known and can be let go without the usual process of eliminating a full-time employee.

Protecting the Culture Through the Way You View Values and Performance

In this section when we use "Values," we are including the entire gamut of Vision, Mission Values (the beliefs of the organization) AND behaviors. The leader's job is to protect these with the workforce and to protect them through the people you hire.

As with the previous section where we discussed **Hire Slowly and Fire Fast**, part of hiring slowly is ensuring there is a fit with your group. All too often a leader will review the person's background, see that they have done the same job before and come to the decision that they can do that same job again here. That is important but may not be important as how they fit with your culture.

Some very high performing companies have taken the approach, "We hire for attitude and train for skill."

Larry Bossidy was one of the most senior executives at GE. Very few organizations are focused on performance as passionately as GE was at that time.

When he left GE to join Allied Signal as their CEO, he made the rounds to the key locations. In his discussions he showed the following grid:

Characteristics Of An Employee		Can Make Their Goals	
		Yes	No
Embraces Our Values	Yes	1	2
	No	3	4

He was reported to say that if an employee were in **Quadrant 4,** he wanted them out of the company by the end of the day (or by the end of his presentation)!

He went on to say that the company certainly wanted employees in **Quadrant 1**–they embrace our values and can make their goals.

He continued to say:

Quadrant 2–If someone is in Quadrant 2, they need to make their goals. The company cannot survive if people do not make their goals. However, the company will coach them, help them, and support what they need to do/change to achieve their goals. They must, however, eventually progress so they can make their goals.

Quadrant 3–His view was this quadrant is where the problem will be found. Leaders want to overlook the behavior of those who can achieve their goals.

HOWEVER: If these leaders are allowed to stay, they deteriorate the culture (Vision, Mission, Values, and Behaviors) of the organization. Obviously, this cannot be allowed to happen. As painful as it is, they need to leave the organization before they deteriorate the values from within.

I (Walt) now rely on tools from BestWorkDATA to eliminate bad hires from any organizations I'm supporting or working with. The advanced (7th generation psychometrics) tools let us know whether the candidates have the hard-wiring necessary to do the job and the traits required to do it well. For example, we've seen organizations with salespeople that are hard-wired to avoid closing the sale because they don't want to be rejected. It's great to see this in the report from the tool before we hire them for a job that they will never be good at.

Rewards, Awards, and Recognition

Award and recognition programs are a vital component of building your culture and ensuring that you have hired the right people. What your company does to recognize and reward your people also speaks volumes to the employees and key stakeholders, revealing what you really value as opposed to what you say you value in your vision, mission, and values statements.

For the last several years, Walt has used a small but focused set of annual awards to drive the culture in a defined direction.

- Because the company needed great customer service, we recognized individuals for going the extra mile to help satisfy customers by awarding them the *Golden Rule Award*.

- Because we valued reliability and dependability, we recognized individuals for work ethic and showing up with the Ripken Award or the *Iron Man Award.*

- Because we valued the ability to maintain calm and a sense of context when tensions get high, we awarded individuals with the *Cool Hand Luke Award.*

- Because we valued learning and sharing, we awarded individuals who were actively learning and growing and sharing what they learned with the *Einstein Award.*

- Because we value talent and teamwork, we awarded individuals with the *Top Hand Award* for the person on the team that contributed the most to the team's successes.

- Because we valued the heartset and origin of our company, we awarded individuals with the *Founder's Spirit Award* to continue the tradition of entrepreneurial inspiration and creativity in support of our customers.

"True performance excellence in an organization requires the union of operational performance and a culture that supports people and teams to be at their best. Leaders are continuous teamers who genuinely care for the support and development of others."

Astrid Nelson
Deputy General Manager/CAO
Prince William Water

All together, these annual awards, with nominations and voting done by the team, created an environment where everyone knew what our values were, and everyone supported the awards and the winners because they had a voice and role in the selections.

This worked well for me at three different companies and ultimately spread to the larger organizations that we were part of. Celebrating the positives is good.

I've also used an award I called *"The Big Gulp"* to celebrate and share knowledge about mistakes and lessons learned. At a company with many field engineers, we bought a giant Slurpee in the Big Gulp cup, cleaned it and decorated it for less than five dollars, and at our weekly all hands and safety briefings we would hear stories from the field and vote on that week's Big Gulp winner.

This helped promote learning, trying, and knowledge sharing. Interestingly, the engineers really liked having the cup for the week when they won. Celebrating the mistakes reduced the number and certainly reduced the number of unique mistakes for that team.

 Chapter 1 Keys:

Chapter 1: What Is a Leader?

- The source is written for leaders who drive value for their stakeholders.

- Leadership is not as well understood as one might think.

- The book draws upon the authors' experiences in the military and sports to provide clarity and perspective on leadership systems.

- To be successful, leaders must have a systematic approach to leadership, which the book refers to as a Leadership System.

- Leaders must become teachers, effectively communicating knowledge and demonstrating wisdom to their followers.

- Leaders must understand the difference between knowledge, which can be taught, and wisdom, which must be observed.

2

Preparation for Becoming a Leader

Evaluate Your Starting Point

"Drivers: Start your engines!"

What is your "engine" in leadership? I submit that your engine is your team of individuals assigned to you. Every leader needs to understand themselves and understand their team. As obvious as this sounds, it seems like it is rarely done. Successful teams have:

- Clear direction

- Strong relationships

- Shared sense of responsibility

- Defined objectives

- Measures of success

- Diverse ideas, styles

- Open and honest communication

Teams are made up of individuals who have different strengths, skills, personalities. The challenge is to get them to all work together to achieve results. The first step is to know yourself. Understand themselves and how their behavior affects others.

Successful people understand their reactions to other people. They know how to maximize what they do well. They have a positive attitude about themselves that causes others to have confidence in them. Know how to adapt their behavior to meet the needs of other people and particular situations.

Leaders must know themselves and leaders must know the individuals on their team.

War Stories from the Road – Know thyself and to thine own self be true

When Walt was serving in the US Air Force, any full Colonel that might be selected for General was sent to what we jokingly called "Charm School." In reality, the program was designed and implemented by the Center for Creative Leadership and was given a cool codename of "Project Looking Glass." The intent of the program was to spend a week evaluating the senior officer in a simulated command setting. While he or she is presented a number of scenarios in the setting, surrounding the "office" are a bevy of behavioral scientists, psychologists, psychotherapists, etc., all looking through the two-way mirrors and taking notes furiously about the senior officer's responses to the scenarios and actors in the simulation. The outcome of this is a massive three-ring binder presented to the senior officer on completion. This is an incredible opportunity to gain great self-awareness. John has one of those binders and it is quite an impressive set of observations and insights. This is a very expensive program. Can you gain these kinds of insights on your leadership style in a less expensive way? Yes. There are many tools available that are much less expensive and, increasingly, less dependent on gathering an army of observers and analysts.

A short list of tools available might include:

- DiSC Profile™

- Myers Briggs Profile™

- Strengths Finder™

- Blake Mouton™

- Banding People Together™

- Best Work DATA™

- Center for Creative Leadership's "Looking Glass" simulation.™

- Kolbe A™

There are several others. The key here is understanding what you need from the tools. A leader needs to know himself or herself:

strengths, weaknesses, tendencies, etc. A leader also needs to know his or her team's individual strengths, weaknesses, tendencies, and much more.

I (Walt) have taken all of those assessments above and now recommend to all of my clients and colleagues the most advanced psychometric tools from Best Work DATA–seventh generation and extremely accurate with over 600 different reports and usage models. The DATA provides profound insights and leads to better hires, better growth and development of both the individual and your teams.

Your organization will, typically, have individuals with all kinds of characteristics in it and you must pull them together and not lose anyone's contribution.

Frequently leaders either don't use people where they can contribute the most, or feel their staff are on the wrong course because of their natural profile. It is easy to:

- Hire only in your own image

- Make leadership decisions not considering all preferences in the organization

- View "different" as defective–when it is only a difference in their profile preferences

- Not realize that these approaches are tools, and any person can change their behavior for a particular event or reason.

- Each profile has a tendency, a way they behave under pressure, and a way they behave under extreme pressure

Culture: Organizational Beliefs and Behaviors

Organizational Behavior and Guidance

Many times, leaders view their "leadership" as impacting themselves and their direct reports – or one or two levels down. NO! The behavior and guidance must go down to every employee.

This means you must have a specific process for ensuring that every employee, at every level, knows and supports the accepted behaviors.

A simple statement to explore this could be: "Show me the new employee orientation." Does it include a clear understanding of our team's behaviors? Even if there are several levels in the corporation above you, you can still set, deploy, and improve the culture in your group.

It must be so pervasive that it can be felt when you walk into the building. It must be guidance for all employees, and it must be felt by visitors, customers, or others you deal with.

The Impact of Culture

Ted Bauer, a "culture commentator," put out an article[3] with this list of bullets on the importance of culture in the business ecosystem:

Culture has become increasingly important, even to execs, in the past decade. Some of the notable findings around culture tying back to the business include:

- 94% of executives believe that a distinct workplace culture is important to their business.

- Strong cultures are associated with 20% higher productivity and significantly less turnover.

- 13 companies have appeared on every edition of *Fortune's* 100 Best Companies To Work For, and those 13 companies outperform the market by 495% annually.

- 88% of job seekers consider the culture a top priority in their search.

- An average employee is 26% more likely to leave their job as the result of a bad culture. (That percentage has been shown in some studies to be *higher* for executive talent, who often have more options.)

---

[3] Ted Bauer article link: Tying "Data" To "Company Culture" - by Ted Bauer

- <u>32% of jobseekers</u> would take a $10,000 pay cut on compensation package for a perceived great culture.

- <u>38% of American employees</u> define culture and a purpose within the culture as key to their work and retention.

We know culture is a big deal, and a defining feature of modern organizations.

But, um, what exactly *is it*?

Deloitte has long been a leader in the research space for culture and engagement, and even they admit that only <u>28% of executives understand what "culture" means</u>, and only 12% believe their company has a strong culture that's aligned with getting the best talent.

What is expected as "High Performance"?

Every organization has a different definition of what constitutes "High Performance." As a leader you need to understand your organization's unique expectation and ensure your team also does.

Some organizations "sugar coat" their problems and are convinced they are always high performing. These organizations will probably struggle to survive in the future.

Other organizations (Believe us. This is true.) are focused on high performance and performance improvement so stringently that you could report:

- The highest performance your group has ever had

- The highest performance in the company

- The highest performance in your industry

You finish your presentation and sit down--your career in that company just ended, and the only one who doesn't know it is you! Why? That company is so focused on improvement that every presentation of current performance is only one-half of what is expected. The other half is *your improvement plans to be even better*.

Every leader should focus on tangible improvement. This starts with defined processes. You can't improve something (and retain that improvement over years and different users) before it is clearly defined.

Processes need to be:

- Defined

- Measured

- Stabilized

- Improved

And it needs to be in that order. Otherwise, you wind up with employees and other key stakeholders who are like our list of troubling drivers from the opening chapter of the book: lost, distracted, unnecessarily aggressive, etc.

Chapter 2 Keys:

Chapter 2: Preparation for Becoming a Leader

- Before becoming a leader, you must understand the organization's vision, mission, values, and culture.

- Leaders must know their own strengths and weaknesses and understand how they affect others.

- Processes must be defined, measured, stabilized, and then improved.

3

What You Lose When You Become a Leader

It is only natural to be proud when you have been recognized and given a leadership position. Suddenly we all seem to temporarily forget all the characteristics of leaders we have followed, which we did not like or respect.

Our thoughts jump to what we now have the freedom to do now. Rarely do we pause and think about all the things we sacrifice when we become a leader. Nevertheless, there are several things you lose.

It's important you know these losses and behave accordingly:

- **You lose the luxury of only thinking only about yourself**

  o Before you were selected as the leader your primary focus was on your own needs and objectives. Sure, you would help a teammate, but that was a secondary issue and would not take precedence over your own needs and objectives.

- o The moment you became a leader you lost that luxury. Suddenly the needs of the team and the teammates on the team became #1. Ask a leader what the needs are for each teammate and the answer will quickly tell you if their team's needs are most important.

- **You lose the ability to openly complain about the organization**

  - o When a leader complains about the organization everybody who can hear them thinks, "Why don't you do something about it? Don't just complain."

  - o You still have the same knowledge about the opportunities to improve, but your role has changed– you need to do something about it. Your team knows your complaints before you become the leader, and they will be watching/waiting to see what you do.

  - o What you can do on this front is ask others about your ideas to improve and get their ideas. Warning: When they tell you their ideas, you must listen and prove to them you are listening.

- **You lose the ability to start/engage in rumors**

  - o Every organization has rumors–some true, some untrue. Although it's not a great characteristic, most of us have "chatted around the water cooler" during our workday. As a leader, participating in this can erode respect for you almost instantly. The rule is simple–don't do it.

o Some leaders have "started a rumor" to see where it comes back, or who, in their organization spreads them. Although this may have limited success, it's really risky.

- **You lose the ability to see a problem and ignore it**

    o As with the above items, you lost this ability when you became a leader. When you see a problem, you should think about what "bucket" it goes into:

    - **Type 1 Problem:** A problem which is timeless and may never be fixed
      Explain why the time, resources, and team energy would be better used elsewhere

    - **Type 2 Problem:** A problem which is difficult and will take a lot of time/effort to fix
      If this type of problem is key to the team's success, a plan should be developed

    - **Type 3 Problem:** A problem which should be addressed quickly
      Put a plan together, or make an assignment and follow-up on the progress

    - **Type 4 Problem:** A "problem" which is not really a problem and should be ignored

Explain to the team why this is the case

Obviously, you can't fix every type of problem quickly, or even fix it at all, but if your leadership is to be viewed as proactive, you need to identify the problem type and act accordingly.

- **You lose the right to not listen to (and understand) the concerns of others in your group**

  o Nothing deteriorates a leader's respect quicker than the team feeling the leader does not care about them. This begins with listening and understanding their concerns.

    - This does not mean you are "nosey" and seek feedback which is none of your business. It does mean when the workforce has a problem you listen to them and do what you can.

  o Everybody understands whether someone is listening to them and whether that person cares about them.

  o In simple terms, "If my boss does not care about me, why would I care about them?"

- **You lose the right not to show gratitude to others.**

  o We have all helped someone who wasn't grateful, and there is very little incentive to ever help them again.

  o As described in the concept of the Second Line previously, when taking over a leadership position it's critical to determine which individuals and groups you should have a good relationship with. If your predecessor had a better relationship with these influencers than you are willing or able to develop, it will eventually catch up with you.

YEARS AGO, ON A TOUR OF PERU, AT EACH LOCATION THE HOSTS ARRANGED FOR A LOCAL SHAMAN TO BE WITH US.

SHAMAN: A PERSON REGARDED AS HAVING ACCESS TO, AND INFLUENCE IN, THE WORLD OF GOOD AND EVIL SPIRITS, ESPECIALLY AMONG SOME PEOPLES OF NORTHERN ASIA AND NORTH AMERICA.

THE SHAMAN AT OLLYATAMBO, PERU TOLD US, "THE MOST POWERFUL EMOTION A HUMAN CAN HAVE IS GRATITUDE."

WHETHER YOU VIEW THAT AS RIGHT OR WRONG, MOST WOULD ARGUE THAT GRATITUDE IS A CRITICAL EMOTION. WHEN SOMEONE HELPS YOU—WINNERS SAY, "THANK YOU."

THAT IS RESPECT AND RECOGNITION FOR WHAT THEY HAVE DONE FOR YOU, AND AN INCENTIVE FOR THEM TO HELP YOU AGAIN.

- **You lose the right to "pass the buck" on decisions.**

  o Every leadership position has a set of decisions, which go with it.

    - You are not expected to make every decision, even CEOs need to go to their Board of Directors above a certain approval level. You are expected to make those decisions that are clearly within your scope and authority.

      We've all seen leaders who cannot or will not make key decisions. They try to pass them up or down and are viewed as being ineffective.

"I believe in consensus, and I work with my team on consensus. However, we will leave this meeting with a decision. If they can't make it I will."

Lee Iacocca

---

o Consensus is great–get opinions. If there is no consensus you are being paid to decide.

o If you want to understand the impact of your decisions, go to your mentor (described later in this book) within your organization.

WE WORKED WITH A CEO WHO MANAGED A **40,000**-PERSON COMPANY. HE DID NOT FEEL HE NEEDED A SYSTEMATIC LEADERSHIP SYSTEM...

THEN A **$5** DECISION CAME ACROSS HIS DESK. HE BECAME PASSIONATE THAT EVERY LEADER AT EVERY LEVEL SHOULD MAKE DECISIONS WITHIN THEIR SPAN OF INFLUENCE.

HE WENT ON TO SAY THAT IF YOU DID NEED TO PASS THE DECISION UP TO YOUR BOSS, YOU SHOULD ALSO REPORT:

- THE PROS OF THE DECISION
- THE CONS OF THE DECISION
- A RECOMMENDATION

THE REALITY IS--IF YOU KNOW THE PROS, CONS, AND A RECOMMENDATION, YOU CAN MAKE MANY OF THE DECISIONS YOURSELF.

- **You lose the right to communicate ineffectively, or not communicate at all**

  o If a leader cannot effectively, AND CLEARLY communicate they should not have been chosen as a leader in the first place!

o This cannot be delegated by leaders at any level. If you think you have communicated clearly, ask someone in your organization to tell you what you have communicated/decided.

- If they communicate the appropriate message, then you have done your job.
- If they can't you need to simplify and clarify your message.

o What you think you communicated may not be what they heard, and certainly may not be what they understood.

It is almost impossible to verify the effectiveness of your communication too much.

- **You lose the right to have a "public" time-out.**

o As a leader you don't get those. You cannot be a role model if everyone knows when you go into a certain business or establishment you don't act like a role model.

- We've all seen US Presidents who (thinking they are "on their own time") want a time-out where their behavior doesn't count.

o In today's world you can assume that the majority of the time, and at any location, your actions and words can be recorded. Once recorded, they are captured forever.

o You have lost the ability to "act out" even though you are not with your team at the time.

- **You lose the ability to (overly) socialize with the team**

    o As the leader your support can be compromised if the team thinks you favor some of the members of the team. If everybody knows "ZZZ" is your buddy, you have compromised the team effectiveness.

    o You can do things with the team as a whole but be very careful not to send a message that some individuals on the team are more important (or better friends) than others.

    o You have lost the ability to *overly* socialize with the team–even if it doesn't bias your views, you will be perceived as being biased.

- **You lose the ability to send the wrong signals**

    o Many of the limitations (losses) listed above are focused on the leader sending the wrong signals.

    o Everybody knows what the boss values.

        - If the leader doesn't live the behavior standards– they don't count.

        - If the leader doesn't enforce the behavior standards–they don't count.

- If the leaders' facial expression is painful when they hear bad news, the organization will no longer bring them bad news, etc.

AS A **CEO** OF A MAJOR COMPANY STOOD IN THE FACTORY LOOKING AT A LARGE BOARD OF METRICS.

JOHN SAID TO HIM IN JEST, "YOU ARE NOT REALLY READING THESE METRICS."

HIS ANSWER WAS STUNNING, AND SHOWED HE CLEARLY UNDERSTOOD THE IMPACT OF HIS ACTIONS, WHEN HE SAID, "I KNOW I'M NOT, BUT EVERYONE IN THIS FACTORY IS WATCHING ME."

EVERYBODY IN THE FACTORY KNEW THE **CEO** LOOKED AT THEIR METRICS BOARD.

IT IS ALMOST IMPOSSIBLE TO VERIFY THE EFFECTIVENESS OF YOUR COMMUNICATION TOO MUCH.

IN A PREVIOUS JOB WE HAD WON A CONTRACT TO DO A LOT OF WORK REPAIRING EQUIPMENT FOR ANOTHER COMPANY.

AS THE HEAD OF PLANNING, I WAS SPENDING DAY AND NIGHT TRYING TO FIGURE OUT WHERE WE WOULD GET THE QUALIFIED WORKERS (FEDERAL LICENSES WERE REQUIRED) TO DO THE NEW WORK.

DURING THIS PERIOD, I WENT DOWN TO A SHOP FOREMAN'S MEETING (25 PEOPLE OF THE 3,000 PEOPLE IN THE WHOLE SHOP). AS I SAT AND LISTENED TO QUESTIONS FROM THE WORKFORCE, ONE OF THE CONCERNS WAS, "I HEARD WE WON THIS CONTRACT, AND THEREFORE THERE WILL BE LAYOFFS."

I WAS FLOORED BY THIS! THAT WAS 100% THE OPPOSITE OF WHAT I HAD BEEN WORKING ON!

I ASKED THE FOREMAN IF I COULD ADDRESS THAT CONCERN.

HOW IN THE WORLD DID THE FACTS GET THAT DISTORTED? CLEARLY, WE HAD NOT DONE AN ADEQUATE JOB OF COMMUNICATING WHAT COULD HAVE BEEN A MOTIVATIONAL MESSAGE: "WE VALUE YOUR SKILLS SO MUCH WE WANT TO HIRE MORE PEOPLE WITH THAT SKILL."

Chapter 3 Keys:

Chapter 3: What You Lose When You Become a Leader

- When you become a leader, you lose the right to think only about your own needs.

- Leaders lose the right to "pass the buck" on decisions.

- Leaders lose the right to communicate ineffectively or not at all.

SECTION 2

Culture & Systematic Leadership

4

A Culture Ready to Change?

When David Spong moved from Airlift and Tanker to Aerospace Support, 95% of his new leadership team had not been through the performance excellence (Baldrige) process. They were not really in favor of the journey and did not clearly see the benefits.

At a key leadership offsite with approximately thirty leaders they asked, "Isn't it very expensive to do this?"

David's response was brilliant when he said:

- "Yes--It's very expensive to run a high-performing organization."

While the room was silent, he continued and said:

- "But it's much more expensive to run a low-performing organization."

How Good Do You Think Your Organization Is?

Does your ego or someone else's on the team get in the way of progress?

We have an exercise we use with leadership teams:

We ask:

Write down 1, 2, 3, 4 on a sheet of paper, and independently answer these questions using a 1 (none) to 10 (lots) scale:

1. What is the need for the overall organization to improve?

2. What is the need for the organization, division, or group you lead to improve?

3. What is the need for you to improve?

4. What one word describes how you felt inside the last time somebody looked you in the eye and said, "You need to improve?"

What we typically see is the individual average and range of answers for 1, 2, and 3 get lower as you go down. What this tells us is the leaders believe, 'The organization needs to improve, and obviously the other leaders need to improve, but I'm OK.'

In decades of doing this worldwide, we have only seen two companies where the number became larger as you go from 1 to 3. One was in Bangalore, India, and the other was in Atlanta, Georgia.

Also, three quarters (or more) of the words used in number 4 are negative. What this tells us is the discussion of improvement, or telling someone they need to improve, OR MORE TO THE POINT--SOMEONE TELLING YOU THAT YOU NEED TO IMPROVE is a negative feeling and experience. That's certainly not something you will look forward to doing.

Another question we always ask is: "If you have two organizations, and one has lots-and-lots of problems and the other organization doesn't have any problems, which one is low performing, and which one is high performing?" Usually this is an interesting conversation, and most groups have a mixed response.

Our experience is clear—the organization with lots of problems will **always** be higher performing.

Why?

The high performing organization is more proactive in identifying their problems, and once they identify them, they immediately work on improvements. Typically, these organizations also have problem-solving techniques which they systematically use across all employee groups or departments. They do not delegate improvement to one staff group, but teach everybody the tools, and then expect them to use them.

The organization which doesn't think they have any problems has just as many problems as the high performing organization, but they don't know what they are, and they are not working to discover them or fix them.

If you ask most leaders how good their organization is (on a 1–10 scale) many will tell you a 10. Why not? They have worked all their life to get here.

Reflecting on the graphic below:

- The more you know about world class performance, and the more you have the humility to be honest with yourself, the lower your opinion of your performance–you know more about what is possible.

- To this point–years ago we were at a health care conference and handed out a questionnaire. One question, asked to over 300 people–looked for how much they knew about world-class performance (i.e., The Baldrige Criteria), and another question asked how good they thought their organization was.

INTERPRETING ORGANIZATIONAL MATURITY

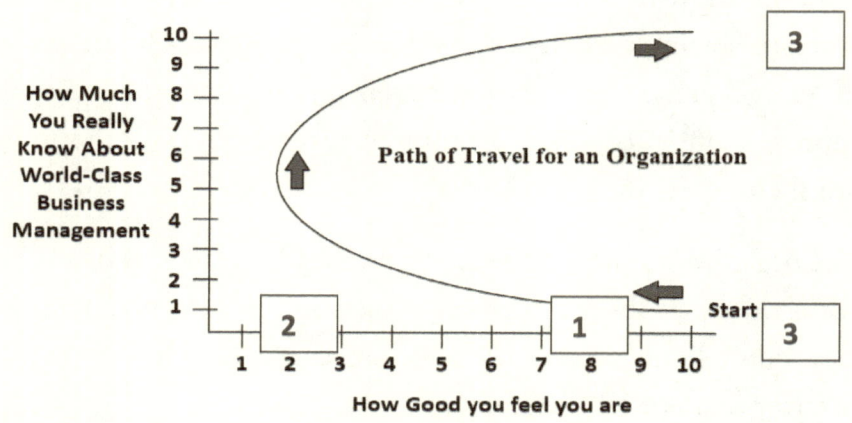

- The more they knew, the worse they thought their organization performed–See Danger Area 1, below.

When leaders (or others) start learning about world-class performance their opinion of themselves starts to crash. The danger areas, typically, are:

Danger Area # 1

- We're Starting to learn--This is tough!

- We thought we were a '10' and now we think we are a '6'

- Our self-opinion is crashing

- This 'World-Class Business Management' criteria obviously does not fit us

- Let's try to discredit the source

Danger Area # 2

- We're working hard

- Now we think we are a 2–4 in how good we feel

- We're investing & learning fast

- We're implementing improvements fast

- We ARE improving, but because of the rate of change, our self-opinion isn't improving

Danger Area # 3

- If you think you are perfect (on either end of the C-Curve) your days of improving are over

Our experience has shown that world-class organizations are a 2 or above on the "How good you feel you are" scale, and a 7 or above on the "How much you really know about world-class business management" scale.

This means they stay hungry on the horizontal scale and are always fixing problems rapidly on the vertical scale.

 Chapter 4 Keys:

Chapter 4: A Culture Ready to Change?

- Organizations need a culture that is ready to change, and leaders must assess the organization's readiness.

- A leadership system is the primary tool for shaping an organization's culture.

- Leaders must define and enforce behavioral standards.

- Leaders must identify key decision influencers in their organization.

- Leaders must understand who their "outlaws" (resistant to change) and "pioneers" (change agents) are.

- Leaders must have multiple listening posts to gather information.

5

What Is a Leadership System?

We always marvel when we ask someone if they have a leadership system. The answer is almost always YES, and they begin to describe an organization chart and who-reports-to-who.

An Organization Chart is NOT a Leadership System, and this evokes several thoughts:

- They have no idea what a leadership system is.

- All organizations have a reporting structure, and this is not a leadership system.

- The Organization Chart does not teach someone how to lead!

- A set of committees is not a Leadership System.

This book will show you what a leadership system is, how to use it, and how to develop your own. We do not suggest that any one of the examples of leadership systems we present is the one you will eventually adopt. One size does not fit all, and your leadership system is not something you can "borrow" from another group or as we suggested up front – borrow from another leader. Your organization's unique context and your people should shape your culture. Your leadership system is the primary tool you and your current (and future) people will use to shape that culture in an intentional manner.

The leadership systems shown are only examples and can be used as a starting point for you to develop your own systematic approach to leadership, put in your own style and that of your team, and tailor to the culture of your company, your business, and your group of stakeholders.

That is why we have a set of steps in the Appendix showing you how to develop your own Leadership System.

Below is an example of the concept of a Leadership System. As David Spong says in his Foreword–this is a very simplified version of what his team developed in their early years.

Very Simple Leadership System

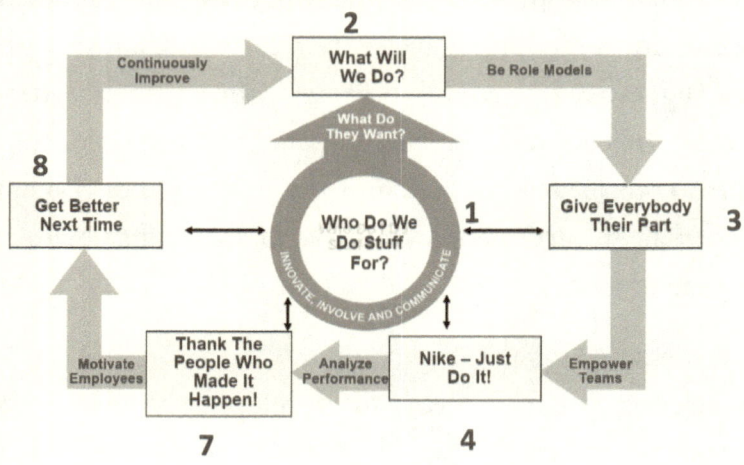

5 -Perform
6-Measure Performance

In this Leadership System the symbols 1 through 8 are used, and those same symbols are used throughout this book. They refer to the Leadership System sections shown above. This will be significantly expanded in Chapter 7 where we discuss a more mature Leadership System, its use, and add more nuance in the sections shown above.

The leader must plan each step to close the gap.

VISION is critical. With a vision and a plan to close the gap between the current state of the organization and that visionary aspiration, the leaders can and must adjust in accordance with the vision and plan. Without a vision, and without a plan, what happens in most organizations?

War Stories from the Road – Strategic Challenges

What are your strategic challenges? What's coming at you from the outside? What are your critical success factors? What do you have to be good at? What are you good at? What's changing in your marketplace?

I (John) heard Jim Collins talk one time. He says, "Everyone in the same marketplace has the same luck. It's what happens in the marketplace. Winners do something with it, losers don't. You get your strategic objectives; you get your actions. Then you put systems together."

At a conference several years ago, I followed John Timmerman to the podium. Believe me, if there's ever anything you don't want to do in life, you don't want to follow John Timmerman to the podium talking about leadership. It'd be like going to the podium and speaking on spiritual issues following Mother Teresa. I talked to John ahead of time, got his presentation and segued my presentation with his. He had already said, "Roughly fifty percent of employees know what's expected of them."

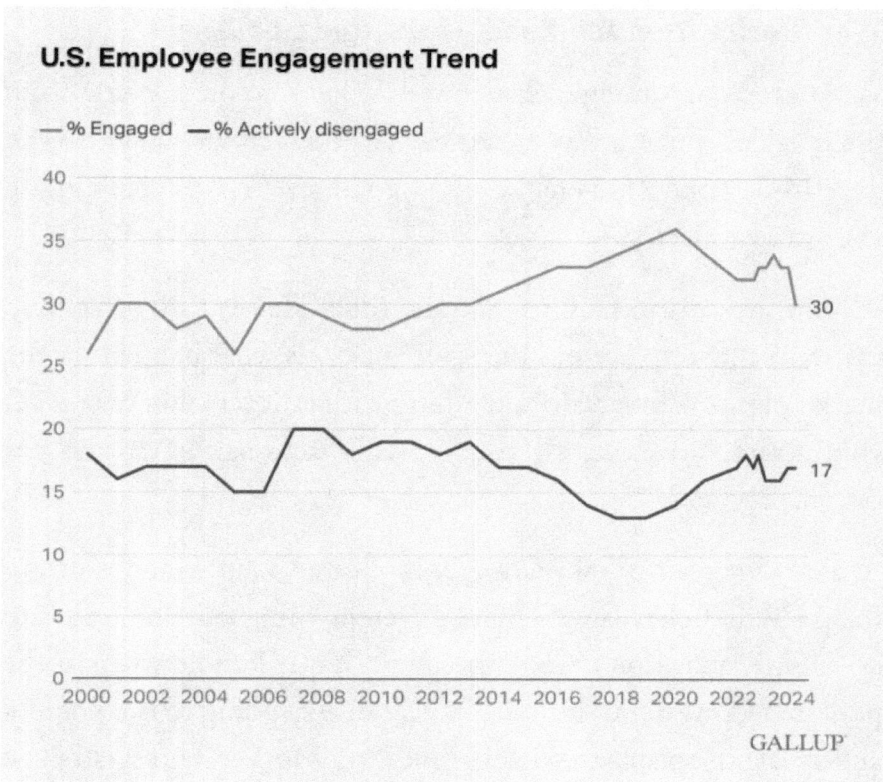

I mean, that's mind boggling. At the time John Timmerman oversaw research for Gallup, but the first thing that jumps into your accounting mind is half the money you're paying for salaries is a waste. But more importantly, what's the impact of that on the other 50%?

For example, I literally remember being in my office thinking to myself, "I wonder if Alan's working hard today? I wonder, he doesn't seem to be working that hard." Well, that's a stupid question. If I don't first ask, does Alan understand the organization's objectives? Does he understand his objectives?

Does he understand the impact of his objectives on the organization's objectives? Because if he doesn't understand those, it doesn't make any difference if he's working hard.

In my experience, "Alan" may be working hard and doing something he's very passionate about with great energy. Unfortunately, that effort may be completely out of alignment with the vision, mission, values, and goals of the organization. Worst case, the effort is not just misaligned--it may be counterproductive. In many organizations, the "Alans" don't know what is expected of them, but believe they must be busy doing SOMETHING. It's the same reason dogs chase cars–I must be on the porch for some reason, right?

Getting The Team on The Same Page

Leaders Often:

- Want everybody to have the same skill set

- Don't recognize the talents of each person, which are unique to the team

- Don't understand how to leverage the unique talents of each person

- Don't understand how to blend the talents

Having the same skills is never the goal and a key job of a leader is to use all the talents on the team. This requires everyone to recognize and adhere to the rules of the team.

Organizations, typically, have a Vision, Mission, and Values (VMV) -- their core merits being:

Vision

The term "vision" refers to the desired future state of your organization. The vision describes where the organization is headed, what it intends to be, or how it wishes to be perceived in the future.

Mission

The term "mission" refers to the overall function of an organization. The mission answers the question, "What is this organization attempting to accomplish?" The mission might define customers or markets served, distinctive or core competencies, or technologies used.

Values

The term "values" refers to the guiding principles and behaviors that embody how your organization and its people are expected to operate. Values reflect and reinforce the desired culture of an organization. Values support and guide the decision making of every workforce member, helping the organization accomplish its mission and attain its vision in an appropriate manner. Examples of values might include demonstrating integrity and fairness in all interactions, exceeding customer expectations, valuing individuals and diversity, protecting the environment, and striving for performance excellence every day.

More concisely:

Vision

What do we want to be in the future?

Mission

What do we do each day?

Values

What are our underlying beliefs?

These are the overarching beliefs or desires of the organization.

None of these, however, are of value unless they drive the actual **behaviors** of the leader and everyone on the team.

It's easy to find examples of organizations who have lofty VMV that do not act that way. As a customer you can almost see this contradiction daily.

Culture

What's the price for not doing this?

Here's a post from author Tom Goodwin to LinkedIn in 2024, describing his view of the landscape:

I think I sit in meetings about 40 times a year where it seems obvious that:

1. Things are not as complex as people make out.

2. We are measuring the wrong things.

3. Everyone is really smart, experienced, motivated.

   And

4. A lot of really quite stupid things are being done.

As individuals people always seem amazing, but put them together into a committee, department, or business, and somehow it just seems to go wrong.

We see this in Politics, in Government, in large companies and in nimble trendy small ones.

I really wish companies could focus on

1. How to make small changes to build organizational change muscles.

2. Reducing complexity and making things simple

3. How to stop doing dumb stuff.

4. How to focus on what actually matters.

5. How to really measure what matters.

As technology allows us to do more and more stuff, let's use it to focus on simplicity and focus, not on simply allowing us to be more busy, chasing more data and more distractions from the tasks at hand.

Does this resonate with you?

How many of the research findings asserted below do you know in your heart are probably true:

- According to exit interviews conducted over many years, the CHRO reports that the number one reason that companies lose people, and the attrition number increases, is because they have bad leaders/bad managers micromanaging their people.

  o 82% of your managers are not good at leading people.

    - Corollary: The other 18% are carrying a heavy responsibility and may be overloaded.

  o This is one reason why so many transformations fail.
  o This is a factor why so many projects fail.
  o This is why so many of our employees are checked out and disengaged. And yet, we're not doing anything to fix that. Why?

- Gallup studies have shown that at least 50% of employees do not know what is expected of them!

Fixing the culture is not the only thing a leader needs to do, but it is the first thing!

Even if you don't lead the corporation, you are responsible for the culture in the group you lead. The culture is sitting there waiting for you. Whether you are promoted from within or recruited as the new leader, you will find that there is an existing culture. It may be the kind of culture that eats your strategy for breakfast, lunch, and dinner–the kind where the group you are now leading will respond to your leadership with statements like, "That's not the way we do things here." That is a statement of culture. This statement is essentially a call to battle. The behaviors that you tolerate will be seen in ever-growing numbers, good and bad. If you can identify the aspects of the existing culture that are good or great, you can anchor into these to help change the other aspects that are not supportive of your vision.

We know from many years of experience that you are not going to "fix" the decayed or decaying culture without effective leadership at every level of the organization. At the end of the book, we present an afterword by a leader who did not inherit the culture he wanted, and you can read his story of how he transformed the culture to achieve high performance and growth.

An iceberg graphic which shows this relationship is:

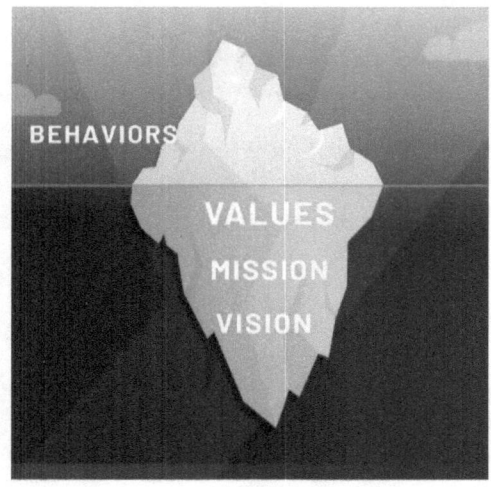

> *"If I could start my role as a leader over, I would take more time to listen."*
>
> **Lee Butler**
> **Don Chalmers Ford**
> **Performance Excellence**
> **Malcolm Baldrige National Quality Award Recipient**

What everyone sees in an organization AND in your leadership are the behaviors which are demonstrated and accepted or tolerated.

In an appendix are three examples of organizations who clearly defined, implemented, and lived their behaviors:

- Lafayette General Medical Center's Standards of Behavior (an entire organization)

- Boeing Aerospace's Operating Principles (a group within a larger organization)

- Sharp Healthcare's Behavior Standards (an entire organization)

Also included in the appendix is a presentation of the US Air Force Code of Values, another example of precise statements of behavior standards–note these are all explicit, none of the examples are implicit (unspoken).

Each of these, when fully executed, provides guidance for group behavior, team behavior, and individual behavior. As discussed in the Leadership System chapter, no leader can fail to be a role model. If you don't follow your team's behavioral guidelines, why should anybody else?

Vision, Mission, and Values are WORTHLESS unless you clearly define, measure, and hold yourself and your organization's members accountable to the supportive behaviors. If someone violates your established behaviors, they may not fit in the organization. You, as the leader, cannot delegate the responsibility to enforce behavioral standards.

Most organizations don't go further than just their Vision, Mission, and Values. Trust us– everybody won't synthesize these the same way or use the same standards for how they will be accountable to behave. These MUST be clearly translated further into:

- **Behaviors**: What behaviors are/are not condoned?

- **Tactics**: How have you taught each behavior, or how has the behavior been driven into the organization?

- **Measures**: How do you track each behavior in training or reality?

The graphic below shows how an organization focusing on a specific criterion was able to align everybody to the team's objective.

With this alignment everybody is focused on the organizational goals.

Without this alignment, everybody is focused on their own interpretation of the goals. These rarely mesh with the overall objectives or team/organizational goals.

Aligning The Focus (A Typical Organization)

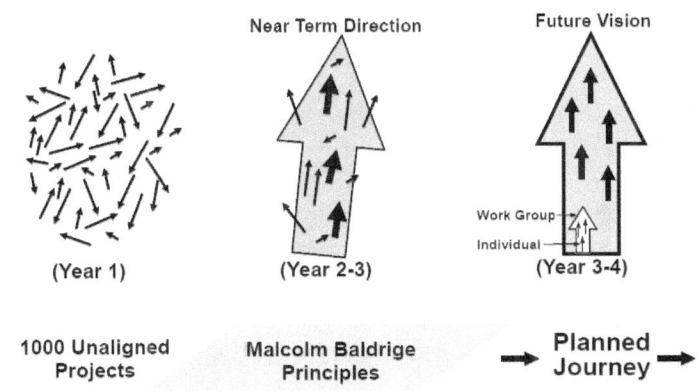

Adapted From David Spong, Boeing Airlift and Tanker

Who Supports Your Teams Success? The "Second Line"

There is a concept in New Orleans called the "Second Line." If you are invited to go to a wedding or funeral you dress accordingly, and frequently participants carry an umbrella. The umbrella signifies you are an invited guest (the First Line).

If you see a wedding or funeral go by, however, the culture in New Orleans is to join in the celebration or grieving as the Second Line.

If you see a "First Line" go by, because you did not know this was going to happen today, you are not dressed accordingly, and you do not have an umbrella... you join in anyway and wave a handkerchief or whatever you can.

An important concept for leaders is to know who is in the *Second Line* for your team's success. People or groups outside of yours who support your success need to be known and nurtured. Thinking back on our careers, there were people and teams who were in our *Second Line* who we thanked, but we didn't fully recognize or nurture them.

Additionally, leaders need to be aware of those individuals and groups who need you in their *Second Line*. It can't be a one-way street. Even when we did know who was "on our side," we didn't always clearly understand (because we did not ask), "What do you need from me or my team to help you achieve your goals?"

If you plan on being on someone's *Second Line*, it is key to understand how they are measured. Your actions need to help their measured performance and cannot hurt their metrics.

Think for a moment, who do you want from your supportive organizations (helping you achieve your deliverables and metrics) in your *Second Line?*

Who Should You Develop a Relationship With, and an Understanding Of?

Everybody wants the leader of your *Second Line* to be a supporter. It's unfortunate, however, if you do not also know who the key decision influencers are in that organization, or in your own organization.

They may be even more important than the leader.

Think about your (and your Second Line's) metrics in the following context:

Impact On Your Relationship	Decision Makers	Decision Influencers
Yes	The Group Leader	Possibly The Leaders Deputy
No	Leaders At All Levels	Minimal Impact Individuals

Everybody wants the leader of your supportive group to be "on board." However, consider the following impact based on longevity and influence.

Tenure	Decision Makers	Decision Influencers
Yes	1-5 Years?	Can be 10-20 or more years
No	Various	Various

Typically, what the decision influencer wants to happen will happen. Maybe not under this leader, maybe not under the next leader, but eventually what they want will happen.

One person in that position (referring to the leader of the organization) said:

- "I'm a B employee."

When asked to explain he replied:

- "I *be* here when they (the new leaders) get here, and I *be* here when they leave." In other words, what he wanted to happen WAS going to happen sooner or later.

Additionally, don't forget who briefs the new leader when they arrive on the value of their organization being in your *Second Line*.

YEARS AGO, I (JOHN) WAS THE SENIOR EXECUTIVE IN CHARGE OF MANUFACTURING AND QUALITY, REPORTING TO THE CEO. WHEN I TOOK A TRIP TO VISIT A SPECIFIC ONE OF OUR NINE FACTORIES, I WOULD NOT GO DIRECTLY TO THE PLANT MANAGER'S OFFICE—BECAUSE I CAN SEE HIM ANY TIME.

INSTEAD, I WOULD GO INTO THE FACTORY AND STAND AT LOUIS'S MACHINE AND TALK TO HIM FOR AS LONG AS HE WANTED TO TALK.

HE WAS NOT ON AN ORGANIZATION CHART ANYWHERE, HE WAS NOT A UNION STEWARD, HE WAS NOT ANYWHERE IN THE UNION HIERARCHY. HOWEVER, WHEN I WAS SITTING ACROSS FROM THE UNION PRESIDENT THE NEXT DAY AND TELLING HIM WHAT WE WOULD LIKE TO DO. GUESS WHAT HE ASKED! "WHAT DOES LOUIS THINK ABOUT THIS?"

IF LOUIS LIKED THE IDEA, WE WERE "GOOD TO GO." IF HE DID NOT, IT WASN'T GOING TO HAPPEN. IF YOU DIDN'T KNOW HIS OPINION, THE MEETING WITH THE UNION PRESIDENT WAS JUST WASTING EVERYBODY'S TIME.

IT IS CRITICAL FOR LEADERS TO UNDERSTAND WHO THE KEY DECISION INFLUENCERS ARE IN THEIR ORGANIZATION. AS SURPRISING AS THIS IS, MANY LEADERS DO NOT KNOW THIS.

GET A PEN AND PAPER AND WRITE DOWN WHO YOURS ARE RIGHT NOW OR START THE QUEST TO FIGURE IT OUT.

Outlaws and Pioneers

As you lead it is important to understand who your "outlaws" and "pioneers" are. Without this understanding, you will not achieve your goals and will struggle to understand why you and your team are failing.

Consider this graphic:

Distribution of Attitude

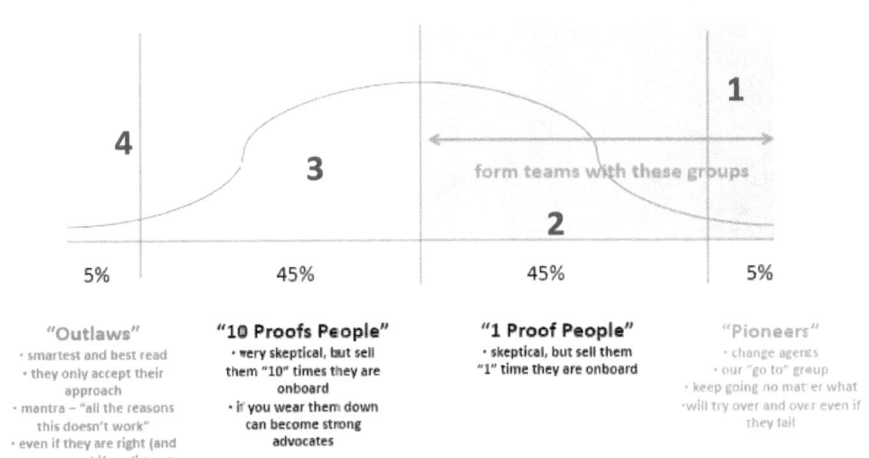

5%	45%	45%	5%
"Outlaws"	"10 Proofs People"	"1 Proof People"	"Pioneers"
• smartest and best read	• very skeptical, but sell them "10" times they are onboard	• skeptical, but sell them "1" time they are onboard	• change agents
• they only accept their approach	• if you wear them down can become strong advocates		• our "go to" group
• mantra – "all the reasons this doesn't work"			• keep going no matter what
• even if they are right (and we are wrong) if we listen to them all progress stops			• will try over and over even if they fail

A small percentage of any organization (approximately 5%) are the 1 **Pioneers**. These are the change agents and as a leader you learn quickly to "go to" these people. They will keep going no matter what, and will try over and over, even if they fail. You just need to recognize their effort and encourage them to try again.

Forty-five percent of most organizations 2 are skeptical of change, but if you show it to them one time (a **1 Proof Person** = 1PP), they are supportive of the changes you are trying to make. Once they are on board, you can give them assignments to help the team, and they will typically respond favorably.

Forty-five percent of most organizations can be very skeptical 3, but if you sell them on the change over and over (a **10 Proof Person** = 10PP) you can wear them down. 10PP's can be very vocal and can be important decision influencers in the organization.

One of the reasons a 10PP can be so valuable is, if you wear them down, they can be a significant bellwether to the entire organization, including other 10PP's. Everybody knew they were previously a skeptic, and will see that your approach must make sense or the 10PP would not have bought in.

We told you that story so we can tell you this one:

Five Percent of the organization are 4 **Outlaws**. In the past we would argue, "We have the right approach to improvement, AND the Outlaw's approach, which is not supportive of our approach, is wrong!"

We've learned over the years that arguing that the outlaws are wrong is not a fruitful battle. A lot of time is expended, and agreement is rarely reached in a manner which everyone, including the Outlaw, follows.

Going forth let's assume this about the Outlaws:

- They are the smartest

- They are the best read

- Their approach is right, or at least better than our approach

Experience has shown that as important as these issues are, **they are not the point.**

Outlaws will only accept their approach and can tell you all the reasons why any other approach, including yours, will not work.

But... if you start to implement their approach, they will always tell you why "the way you are doing it" is not quite right and will ultimately lead to failure unless you make more changes. No matter how or how many times you change, they will always require "just one more" change to be a success.

We want to hear and understand them--they frequently have some good points or perspectives on the change, BUT...

The Point is - - and this is important:

Even if the outlaws are right and we are wrong, if we listen to them, all progress stops. They don't accept the approach of implement, adjust, adjust, adjust, etc.

If you put an Outlaw on a team, the third or fourth team meeting will be to discuss throwing the Outlaw off the team.

You will be the most successful if you form teams starting from the right-hand side of this curve and choose pioneers and 1PP's for your team. You know who the Outlaws are–don't put them on a critical team. Instead, find another way they can contribute.

Pioneers--Willing to try when it's hard and success isn't guaranteed:

> *"It is not the critic who counts; not the man who points out how the strong man stumbles, or where the doer of deeds could have done them better. The credit belongs to the man who is actually in the arena, whose face is marred by dust and sweat and blood; who strives valiantly; who errs, who comes short again and again, because there is no effort without error and shortcoming; but who does actually strive to do the deeds; who knows great enthusiasms, the great devotions; who spends himself in a worthy cause; who at the best knows in the end the triumph of high achievement, and who at the worst, if he fails, at least fails while daring greatly, so that his place shall never be with those cold and timid souls who neither know victory nor defeat."*
> **Theodore Roosevelt**

Inclusion of All Inputs

It is almost impossible to have too many listening posts. As a leader you have the responsibility to have access to information which can drive your success, and it is rare that the needed information comes to you in your office between 9 and 5.

Manufacturing leaders walk the shop floor, accounting leaders network with industry contacts and dig below the high-level numbers, marketing leaders meet with customers, ALL leaders network with their workforce, etc.

In addition to having listening posts, a leader must have listening skills. Some of the most talented leaders still occasionally take training courses in listening.

 YEARS AGO, WE WORKED WITH A FOREIGN COMPANY WHO HAD **3,000** EMPLOYEES. WE WERE FLIP CHARTING THE DIFFERENCE BETWEEN LEADERS AND MANAGERS WHEN THE CEO SAID SOMETHING WHICH WAS SIMPLE, POWERFUL, AND STOPPED US IN OUR TRACKS: "MANAGERS TALK, LEADERS LISTEN."

THAT COMPANY TODAY HAS OVER **300,000** EMPLOYEES.

At a conference recognizing Baldrige Winners, a CEO was asked, "What was the most difficult lesson you and your executive team had to learn?"

His reply was, "Learning to recognize the people who just made us feel bad."

Sitting in the audience, none of us had any idea what he was talking about. He then drew this graphic:

	Unconscious	Conscious
Competent	4	3
Incompetent	1 Personal Blind Spot	2

Idea For Improvement

1. He went on to explain that for any topic a leader has not paid attention to, they could be considered incompetent (1). This was not worrisome to the leader because the leader was unaware of the shortcoming.

2. Moving from Quadrant 1 to Quadrant 2 does not solve anything, but you are now aware of the problem.

3. When an employee (or anyone else) comes to you with an idea, "Hey boss, we need to do xxx." It made you feel bad, BUT they learned that this is where all improvements started. Rather than discipline the person they should reward them. Moving from Quadrant 2 to Quadrant 3 solves the problem, hopefully with repeatable systematic processes that others can follow, and it can be deployed where appropriate.

4. Why do you need to move from Quadrant 3 to Quadrant 4? You already have a solution to the problem? It is like

asking, "Why do professional athletes practice? They can already do the job." The process needs to be quicker, more effortless, and ingrained in muscle memory.

Years later we worked with an Air Force General who had a passion against anything he thought was "whining."

When asked, "General, when somebody takes you across the threshold between Quadrants 1 and 2, how do you separate a good person from a whiner?"

His answer was outstanding in its simplicity and insight when he replied, "That's easy–a whiner wants somebody else to fix it, and a good person will help you fix it."

As a leader, recognize those individuals in your organization who bring you opportunities for improvement and who are willing (or in the case of pioneers–anxious) to be a part of the solution.

> *"Leaders have a responsibility to connect people to a larger purpose, to help them own a piece of something more lasting than themselves."*
>
> *Don Pannell, PE.*
> *Deputy General Manager/COO*
> *Prince William Water*

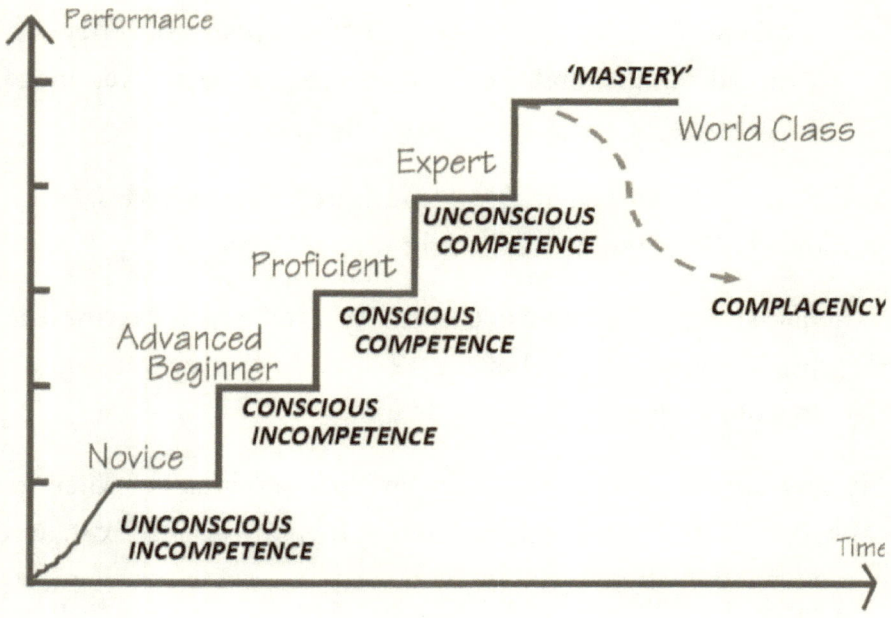

The "Guild" Scale: Novice to Master

From this chart we see another potential danger zone between "Expert" and "Mastery"–the danger of becoming complacent and not continuing to grow in your abilities--even as an expert. Your current level of expertise will, in a remarkably short period, be overcome by the market. One can never rest on yesterday's knowledge and capabilities. It is impossible to drive high performance without continuously improving your own self-awareness and advancing your skills with people.

Driving Performance–Factors

At the beginning of the book, we talked about the different types of drivers we encounter on the roadways. We also noted that many of these drivers are parking in your company parking decks and making decisions as employees or contractors to your team. Are they contributing to "high performance," or are they doing something else?

As we look at the various types of driving behavior, ask yourself, "Where are these folks on the competency charts previously shown? What lack in the leadership area causes these behaviors and what elements of the leadership system shown mitigates, reduces, or prevents these kinds of behaviors in you organization?"

Distracted

Distracted drivers are prioritizing other things over the reason for driving in the first place–to get from one place to another as safely and quickly as possible. If this is the case, what could be the list of reasons why the driver has lost that focus? We've seen drivers here in Atlanta playing endlessly with radio dials/buttons, watching videos on phones, or searching through emails, and oblivious to changing traffic conditions while absorbed in a phone conversation. We can see some drivers with a real book or magazine open on the steering wheel during "rush hour" traffic where everything is crawling. When the distracted (and easily distractable) driver shows up in your company parking lot, how do you keep them focused on work? Do you have people on your team that stay busy but aren't tracking to performance goals? How do you help them regain focus on the mission?

Lost

Lost drivers now have the modern technology in the vehicles and on their phones that should prevent this condition, but we still see them trying to sort out, "Is this really my exit or, do I really need to turn at this light or the next one?"--very localized, very detailed tactical choices, and perhaps a misunderstanding of the instructions from the devices. How do you help these drivers understand the map instructions at a detailed level to avoid the paralysis of indecision? At the time of this writing (mid 2024), most of the navigation tools in use show your location on the moving map, making it incredibly easy to make these decisions. What else might be causing the feeling of disconnectedness? Does your scoreboard and vision map help your team members know they are on the right track? How do you share the vision?

Hesitant/Scared

Hesitant/Scared drivers are a lot like the lost drivers, having a hard time making timely decisions about turns or lanes, but are more dangerous in some ways because, they are also immobilized by the pace and volume of traffic around them, not just the map-related indecision. Afraid of the other drivers (or of making a mistake), they can cause needless slow-downs and traffic jams, because of the lengthy time it takes them to decide and then execute on the decision. How do you and your team help these folks gain confidence in themselves, the team, and the processes and procedures?

Student Drivers

Student drivers are inexperienced. They have no frame of reference and are learning as they go. Because they have very limited experience, they are prone to make decisions and execute them without thinking all the way through potential outcomes. This is why many of them put signs on the cars that say, "Caution, Student Driver. Please be patient." Experienced drivers don't think through choices the way the students do–they can drive based on experience, without consciously making decisions. Not so for the students – they must consider obstacles and options and decide on the best way forward. This takes more time than for the experienced folks and can cause a lack of patience if you are behind them. As you onboard the new employees, how do you set guard rails for them and support systems to ensure their rookie excitement doesn't result in pain for others on the team?

Ancient Drivers

Ancient drivers have loads of experience, but the more experienced they are, the more likely they are to drive without thinking much at all, and they are not armed with the reflexes they may have possessed when younger. This means they "awake to danger" more slowly, and then don't have the resources to respond quickly when the dawning happens. They are still out there on the road, because they are fighting to maintain control and autonomy and don't perceive themselves to be a threat to other drivers. Does your work environment provide a means to engage with these drivers and to help them avoid locking down and instead, keep learning and developing?

DUI

Drivers that have had too much to drink or are under the influence of legal or illegal drugs are some of the most dangerous drivers on the road. Dulled senses and euphoric confidence can lead to real tragedy. Can this happen in a work environment like it does on the roadways? You bet. We've seen it way too many times to discount it. Employees that feel disconnected from the mission, vision, and values of the organization, or, more importantly, that feel disconnected from their leader and team members, sometimes attempt to reduce that painful feeling by indulging in chemistry experiments. At the low end of the spectrum, we've seen folks that take a flask to work and nip throughout the day. At the other end, we've seen hardcore alcoholics that are high functioning, and drug users that mask it decently. These behaviors happen on the roadways… and in the hallways where we work.

Over-Confident Drivers – Racers

There's a related problem in many workforces referred to as the Dunning-Krueger Effect, in which a person really believes deeply that he or she is better, smarter, and more capable than he or she really is based on performance. As a driver, we see them zooming up and by us, using all available lanes and even exit ramps and shoulders to get ahead. These are also the drivers that the law enforcement people are most likely to pull over, as they are most likely to surprise the other drivers and cause an accident. They believe, though, that they are highly proficient drivers and would never believe that they are a risk to others. This is not as unusual as you might think. Researchers have told us that when interviewing individuals and asking them to rate their individual capability or capacity, most individuals rate themselves (on a scale of 1–10, 1 being low and 10 being high) as a 7 or 8. The highest performing folks are the exception and usually rate themselves as a 3 or 4 on the same scale. The reason for this is interesting, as the researchers showed that the massive responder group is comparing themselves to others while the high performers are comparing themselves to their own potential. Wow. How do you think your company's employees would do on this exercise?

Under-Confident Drivers–Tortoises

Tortoises are underconfident for a variety of reasons and are ready to "shell up and stop" in a heartbeat. Extremely defensive drivers create more problems than the Racers. The Racers will find a way to get around the slower drivers and move away quickly. The tortoises are very slow to make lane changes or to enter a high-speed flow of traffic from an on ramp. They frequently tap the brakes as they drive, to make sure they can hunker down quickly if needed. They will also be tapping the brakes while going through a traffic light, in case it turns yellow while they are approaching. They will not run the yellow light. These folks are very rules conscious and risk averse. How do you set a pace and maintain it with the team members that have this driving style?

King of the Road–Rude, Inconsiderate Drivers

Sometimes you see them in the fast lane, driving at the posted speed limit, while traffic is stacking up behind them. They will argue that they are following the law and there is no reason for them to yield, because you should be happy to be going the speed limit. They do not like to be passed, so if you try to go around them on the right, they will speed up to prevent you from getting in front of them. You probably have seen them in your workforce as well. You may have experienced a person who does not like to be challenged in any way and will not be happy for others when they do well enough to be recognized or promoted! Sometimes these "lane rangers" are intentionally holding back other drivers on your team – how do you set up systems to catch this and free those other drivers?

Gracious to a Fault–Unexpectedly Nice Drivers

These folks are not trying to do anything but be helpful to others. However, when they unexpectedly yield to allow someone else to turn in front of them, or to allow someone to cut in front of them, they are breaking the established or "expected, normal pattern" of the roadway. Because these behaviors are not anticipated, they can result in accidents on the roadways. These behaviors in the workplace are also unexpected and can result in similar mishaps. Working together, like driving together, requires everyone to conform to the norms or traditions of shared resources in the office or on the roads.

Backseat Drivers

Critics are often referred to this way. The ones who drive from the backseat are frustrated at their lack of control, and are trying to establish control by suggesting, thinking out loud, or sniping while you are driving the car. At work, these folks are offering what they call "constructive criticism," which is usually neither helpful nor constructive. While they can be annoying, we must remember that we are in fact in control of the vehicle.

Road Ragers – Dangerous, Easily-Triggered Drivers.

Road rage is ugly. Triggered drivers do horrible things to others from an irrational perspective of having been disrespected or devalued by his or her perception of another driver's actions. Their actions are typically seen to be way out of proportion to the triggering behavior from the other driver. Causing an accident that affects many others is certainly out of line. Causing bodily harm or property damage because you got cut off (or passed) is also out of proportion. If your workplace is one that tolerates these irrational ragers, you will see others abandon your hallways quickly. There's no place for this at work (or on the roads).

Conclusion: Drivers of ALL KINDS show up on your workplace roads

One of the best ways to protect your workplace and teams from this group of driving styles is through the thoughtful implementation of a leadership system. The system, much like the lines painted on the roads and highways with good signage, can help smooth the flow and maintain good speed.

 Chapter 5 Keys:

Chapter 5: What Is a Leadership System?

- A leadership system is a systematic approach to leadership, and there are different models of leadership systems.

- Leaders must plan each step to close the gap between the current state of the organization and its vision.

- Leaders must understand stakeholder requirements.

- Vision, mission, and values are worthless unless they drive behavior.

- Leaders must define, measure, and hold themselves and their organizations accountable for supporting desired behaviors.

SECTION 3

Building the System

6

Why Do You Need a Leadership System?

Chapter 7 is why this book has been written.

The next chapter presents a systematic approach to leading, which is frequently called a Leadership System.

Going through graduate school to get a master's degree in management didn't teach me one thing about being a leader.

We:

- Read piles of books

- Philosophized about the characteristics of a leader

- Studied characteristics of organizations

- Studied characteristics of decision-making models

- Studied the importance of change models (although we did not learn how to use them)

- Studied assessment and analysis tools

- Studied financial tools

- Studied statistical analysis tools

It was valuable, but *did not* teach leadership:

1. Focus

2. Actions desired or required

3. Sequence of actions

The key takeaways from this book, however, should be the wisdom of how to use each portion of the leadership system wisely, or the lessons learned from the mistakes of others.

As discussed in the previous chapters, leaders should initiate an entire organization's focus on performance excellence as an effective business tool. For performance excellence to be effective you must (at a minimum):

- Name your processes

- Give the process an owner

- Teach the owner how to:
  - Define
  - Measure
  - Stabilize
  - Improve the process!

- Then you must hold the process owner accountable for process performance and improvement.

If the leaders are not involved in the development and use of the leadership system it will not work as a viable business tool. They cannot delegate the commitment to being the best or to improvement and expect anything tangible or valuable to happen down through the organization. That would be no more foolish than saying, "I hired someone to lose weight for me and they are doing a very poor job."

Everyone in the organization knows what the boss values—look at their calendar and see where they spend their time. Leaders vote on what's important with their calendar. If it is important, they will spend time on it.

Additionally, you can tell what is important to a leader through their expressions. Do they light up when they see improvement? Do they flinch when they hear bad news? Do they ignore problems and let them linger?

Setting Vision and Values

Vision, Mission, Values, and Behaviors (as previously discussed) are critical to your culture. Even if the higher-level corporation has these well established, you can refine them for the group you lead. They cannot conflict with the higher-level corporation, but you can tailor them to your needs, team, and mission.

Clearly, senior leaders must define where the organization is headed, what they want the organization to be, the organization's values (and other beliefs), and acceptable behaviors during the journey.

Frequently the shortcoming is not the lack of values, as many organizations have beautiful plaques on the wall touting a fairly routine set of values or beliefs. The shortcoming is the inability to translate beliefs and values into behaviors and practices, and then the lack of discipline to practice those behaviors each day in every transaction.

As a leader you cannot ignore behavior which is not in keeping with the organization's values, or what is considered legal and ethical. If you do not hold your defined behaviors as sacred, you will be at the mercy of anyone and anything they want to do at any time.

This is where the development of the foundation for a Leadership System is key.

As noted earlier, all too often "Leadership" training is really training in management and has the hope that all students will synthesize the training into the same actions as every other leader—this is a ridiculous expectation.

It is not intuitive what a "systematic approach to lead" might include, but through a clearly defined and implemented Leadership System, the organization can begin to ensure that every leader, at every level, leads in the manner the senior leaders endorse.

IF YOU THINK YOUR ORGANIZATION HAS A CONSISTENT OR SYSTEMATIC APPROACH TO LEADING, WALK THROUGH A CROSS-SECTION OF THE ORGANIZATION AND ASK, "HOW WERE YOU TAUGHT TO LEAD?"

EVERY PERSON WILL GIVE YOU AN ANSWER, BUT ARE THE RESPONSES: 1) CONSISTENT, 2) SYSTEMATIC, 3) IN SYNC WITH THE CULTURE, AND 4) WHAT YOU WANT IN EVERY LEADER?

DO THEY REFLECT THAT EVERY LEADER HAS BEEN TRAINED IN THE SAME APPROACH TO LEADERSHIP AND THE SAME RESPONSIBILITIES?

This, in fact, is a great opportunity for senior leaders to *deploy their wisdom* down to every leadership level.

Sadly, there are billions of dollars spent every year on leadership training when the organization has not even defined their Leadership System, Leadership Responsibilities, Behaviors, or what leaders cannot delegate. This is a waste of money and will not establish a common culture throughout the organization.

Hardwiring the Culture

As previously addressed, the *Vision* is the desired future state, the *Mission* is what we all do every day, and the Values are the guiding principles. These form the organizational beliefs. Most organizations have lofty beliefs and values. The key, however, is the ability to turn these beliefs and values into actions and behaviors. To do this, some organizations have taken the values and translated them into behaviors that are expected of every employee in every transaction with every stakeholder. There are several examples of these in the Appendix.

More advanced organizations have even taken the behaviors and expanded the definition of them to include behaviors that are not acceptable, and how you can recover if you demonstrate one of the unacceptable behaviors.

All *Values* and *Behaviors* are not equal!

Recovery from some behaviors may require a change in your future actions.

- For example: If I did not show a coworker respect, I need to apologize and change my behavior in the future.

Recovery from some other behaviors, however, may be unattainable.

- For Example: Recovery from a breach of integrity may not be possible. The person committing the breach may no longer fit in the organization.

As a leader you may wish to think about and discuss your embedded core beliefs with your team--what you think they are, and what your team thinks they are.

If you have them, they MUST be well communicated, well understood, and cannot be violated in any circumstance.

As you read about a Leadership System in the next chapter, and create your own, ask, **"Does the system that we're building--**

the leadership system in particular--contribute to a restoration of order and a good set of systemically built structures that maintain order over time with less and less actual labor required and more and more fun and creativity required over time?"

IN A BOOK WE PREVIOUSLY PUBLISHED WE DEVELOPED THE TERM "EMBEDDED CORE BELIEF." IT WAS DEFINED AS:

A TERM USED BY SOME ORGANIZATIONS TO DESCRIBE THE ONE BELIEF WHICH IS SO KEY IT IS AT THE TOP OF EVERY THOUGHT, PROCESS, PLAN, MEASURE, AND ACTION. THIS IS PART OF AN ORGANIZATION'S DNA. THIS IS BEYOND CORE VALUES. THIS HELPS GIVE AN ORGANIZATION A SINGULAR FOCUS ON SOMETHING WHICH IS KEY TO THEIR SHORT- AND LONGER-TERM SURVIVABILITY OR DIFFERENTIATION.

FOR EXAMPLE:

- SURVIVABILITY: IN A HEAVY INDUSTRIAL ENVIRONMENT, AN EMBEDDED CORE BELIEF MIGHT BE SAFETY. TO VIOLATE THIS COULD MEAN LOSS OF LIFE IN THE FACTORY.
- ANOTHER EXAMPLE IS DIFFERENTIATION: IN AN INDUSTRY WHICH IS NOT TYPICALLY KNOWN FOR HONEST BUSINESS DEALINGS, THE ORGANIZATION COULD DIFFERENTIATE THEMSELVES WITH "INTEGRITY" AS AN EMBEDDED CORE BELIEF. TO VIOLATE THIS COULD MEAN LOSS OF BRAND IMAGE AND DISTINCTION IN THE MARKETPLACE.

AN EMBEDDED CORE BELIEF IS TYPICALLY AN AREA WHERE VERY LITTLE, IF ANY, EMPOWERMENT IS GIVEN. ORGANIZATIONAL MEMBERS DO NOT CONSCIOUSLY VIOLATE THE EMBEDDED CORE BELIEF AND STAY WITH THE ORGANIZATION. IF THIS INTENTIONALLY HAPPENS, THE DISCONNECT BETWEEN THE ORGANIZATIONAL BELIEFS AND PERSONAL BEHAVIOR WOULD BE MUCH TOO GREAT.

Examples of several organizations' behavior standards and Leadership Systems are shown in the Appendix.

The organization should also be clear about its Core Competency and the relationship to the VMV. The Core Competency is the one thing which drives the organization's competitiveness more than anything else.

Leaders must, at all times, model the behaviors they want to see throughout the organization. When senior leaders do that, they must also ensure that leaders at all levels in the organization are role models themselves 100% of the time for these foundational beliefs to be taken seriously.

WHILE PREPARING AN ORGANIZATION FOR A NATIONAL QUALITY AWARD SITE VISIT, THE LEADER WAS NOT AT A CRITICAL MEETING. KNOWING FULL-WELL WHERE HE WAS, I ASKED, "BILL ISN'T HERE—DOESN'T THAT SEND A BAD MESSAGE?" EVERYONE AGREED, "YEAH, BAD MESSAGE, BAD MESSAGE!" LEAVING THE ROOM QUIET FOR A FEW SECONDS, I LET THAT SOAK IN.

"BY THE WAY, WHERE IS BILL?" IT WAS INCREDIBLE WATCHING THE MOOD IN THE ROOM CHANGE. "OUR MOST IMPORTANT CUSTOMER IS VISITING TODAY. BILL IS WITH THEM."

"WHERE SHOULD BILL BE?"

"WITH OUR CUSTOMER!"

"GOOD MESSAGE OR BAD MESSAGE?"

"GOOD MESSAGE!"

If the leaders do not act as role models all the time, the behaviors and culture changes, and what they desire in the organization, will not take place.

Everyone clearly understands if what the leader says and what they do, or will tolerate, are two different things.

As one Baldrige Recipient CEO put it, "When I asked why the people were not making the changes necessary to transform the organization, the answer I got back was, 'We'll change when the CEO changes!'"

A GREAT STORY ABOUT LEADERSHIP IS TOLD IN INDIA ABOUT GANDHI. IT'S SO WIDELY KNOWN IN INDIA THAT EVERYBODY I KNOW HAS HEARD THE STORY MANY TIMES. TO MY INDIAN FRIENDS, PLEASE FORGIVE THIS INTERPRETATION. I'M SURE ANY OF YOU COULD TELL AN IMPROVED VERSION.

DURING GANDH'S LIFE A WOMAN IN INDIA WAS AT HER WITS END TRYING TO GET HER SON TO QUIT EATING CANDY AND SWEETS. HE WAS OBSESSED WITH THEM. HE WAS OVERWEIGHT, AND THIS OBSESSION WAS GOING TO DESTROY HIS HEALTH.

AS A LAST RESORT SHE ASKED THE BOY, "IF GANDHI TELLS YOU TO QUIT EATING SWEETS, WILL YOU STOP?" THE YOUNG MAN REPLIED, "I RESPECT THAT MAN SO MUCH THAT IF HE TELLS ME TO QUIT, I WILL QUIT!"

FULL OF HOPE THE MOTHER TRAVELED TO MEET GANDHI, TOLD HIM THE STORY, AND GANDHI LOOKED AT THE BOY AND SAID, "COME BACK TO ME IN THREE MONTHS."

THE MOTHER RETURNED HOME WITH HER SON AND WAS SAD THAT HER APPROACH DIDN'T WORK.

BUT... SHE TOOK GANDHI AT HIS WORD, AND THREE MONTHS LATER FOUND OUT WHERE HE WAS, AND TRAVELED ACROSS INDIA AGAIN TO ASK THE SAME QUESTION.

HE LOOKED AT THE YOUNG MAN AND SAID, "EATING SWEETS WILL DESTROY YOUR HEALTH AND I WANT YOU TO STOP EATING THEM FOR ME." INCREDULOUS, THE MOTHER ASKED GANDHI, "WHY COULDN'T YOU HAVE TOLD HIM THAT THREE MONTHS AGO AND SAVED ME A TRIP?"

GANDHI'S REPLY WAS SIMPLE, "MADAM, THREE MONTHS AGO I WAS EATING SWEETS!"

Put more simply, **a leader's actions must speak so loudly that nobody can hear what they are saying.** No leader can get away with the old axiom, "Do as I say, not as I do."

As seen in the flow-down above, from beliefs (Vision, Mission, Values) to behaviors, all employees must understand what the organization stands for, what the organization believes, their personal role, and how they are expected to act. The organizational environment must foster, require, and measure legal, regulatory, and ethical compliance of each leader and every employee. You can't delegate being a role-model.

 Chapter 6 Keys:

Chapter 6: Why Do You Need a Leadership System?

- Leaders should initiate an organization-wide focus on performance excellence.

- Leaders cannot delegate the commitment to being the best or to improvement.

- Leaders "vote" on what is important with their calendar, spending time on what matters.

- A leadership system helps restore order and structure in an organization.

- Organizations should be clear on their core competency list and its relationship to their vision, mission, and values.28

7

A Mature Leadership System

Every aspect of an organization can be systematic–even leadership. As stated earlier, reading tons of management books does not help a leader determine:

1. Focus

2. Actions desired or required

3. Sequence of actions

A Leadership System DOES help a leader understand their role in these factors. Below is an example of a Leadership System, which is used by a high-performing organization.

NOTE: A leader is not only the top echelon of an organization but is any person who has *at least one person* reporting to them.

Every leader at every level is responsible for using the leadership system to lead consistently and fully. They are expected to make

WALT CARTER & JOHN VINYARD

the appropriate decisions required at their level and NOT flow minor decisions or issues up the organization.

Let's Go Through a Leadership System

When most of us think about "Leadership" and our own approach, we don't readily associate it with being a systematic process, where there are steps, measures, and improvement cycles.

The following Leadership System is used by Prince William Water (PWW) in Prince William County, Virginia. A brief description of how it is used by them is discussed in the Appendix.

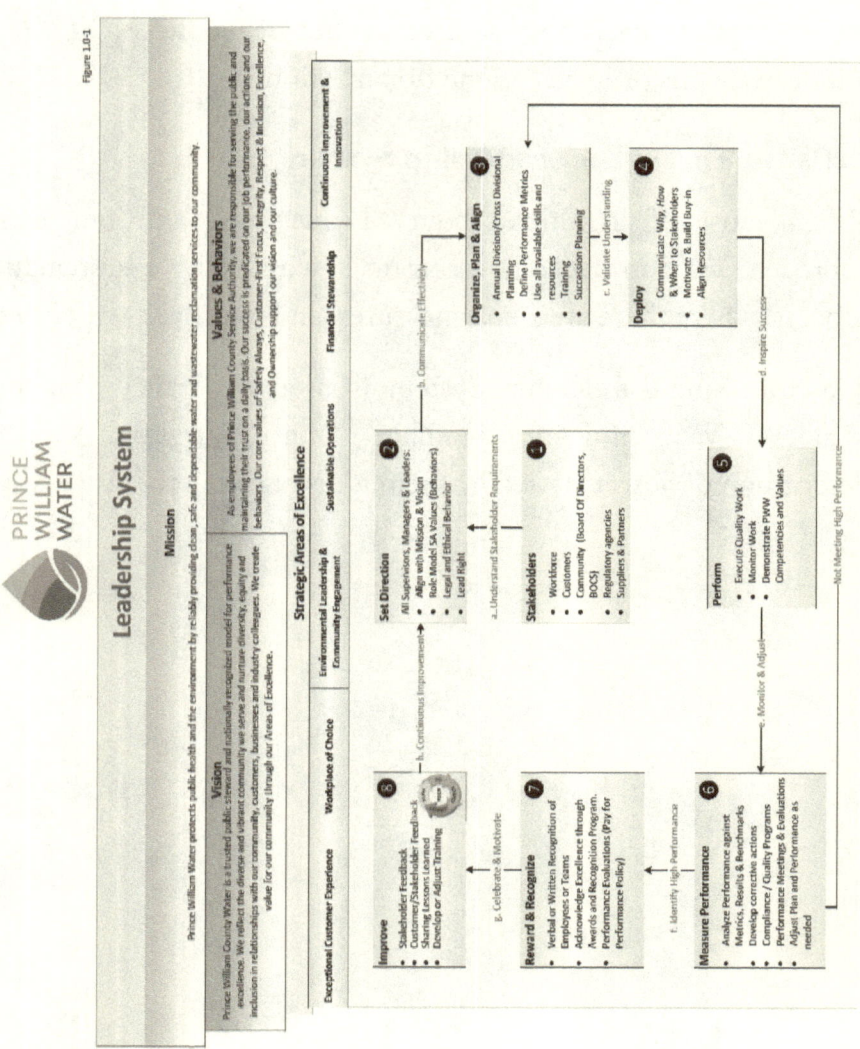

Figure 10-1

This leadership shows the steps to lead (1 through 8, as with the simple Leadership System shown earlier), and the behaviors (notated a through h) are the Vision, Mission, and Values.

NOTE: Values are also identified as behaviors. A mantra we will repeat throughout the rest of this book is that the behaviors (notated a through h AND defined as the other behaviors for all employees in the organization) *cannot be delegated by any leader at any level of the organization.*

Also, in the heading above the PWW Leadership System are the Strategic Areas of Excellence (AOE's), which many Leadership Systems do not include. These remind the Prince William Water leaders what the organization is striving toward and is proud of achieving.

This approach to leadership, leadership development, and leadership deployment provides a roadmap for every leader at every level. This spans from the Board of Directors (BOD) who can set direction for 10 years to the first line supervisor who may only set direction for 10 minutes. BOTH are required to Set Direction.

The Vision, Mission, Values, behaviors, and Strategic Areas of Excellence demonstrate, as discussed earlier, the most important foundation for a leader to establish is culture. This is key, even before step 1 in the Leadership System.

Remember, this is an example of a strong Leadership System and may not fit your organization. Develop your own Leadership System by completing the exercises shown in the Appendix.

Once the foundation of beliefs and behaviors are established, each leader must understand:

Stakeholders

The term "stakeholders" refers to all groups that are or might be affected by an organization's actions and success. Examples of key stakeholders might include customers, the workforce, partners, collaborators, governing boards, stockholders, donors, suppliers, taxpayers, regulatory bodies, policy makers, funders, and local and professional communities.

STAKEHOLDERS: Every leader at every level must engage with their stakeholders to fully understand Stakeholder Requirements.

Frequently leaders strongly feel they already "know" the stakeholder's requirements without any systematic approach to gather what each stakeholder or stakeholder group wants, needs, or requires.

Even if the leader was previously employed by that group, their knowledge is still dated, and what they think are the requirements are still not "owned" by that stakeholder group.

As a leader defines each stakeholder group, they should be careful not to exclude any group, even adding the Second Line.

Stakeholders can include:

- Workforce

- Customers

- The Board of Directors

- The Community

- The boss

- Layers of leaders throughout the organization

- Regulatory Agencies

- Suppliers & Partners

- Collaborators

- Other Departments (Second Line?)

- AND OTHERS unique to your product, service, or organization

For each stakeholder group there needs to be a specific process to collect their needs and requirements, which is validated at the time of collection, and (as you will see later) is revisited throughout the Leadership System.

Assuming you know the stakeholder requirements, without a specific process to identify them can contribute to failure.

You can ask a leader:

- When was the last time you met with each of your stakeholders?

- What is your process to collect their requirements?

- What is your process to validate their requirements?

- What is your process to ensure they agree with what you perceive as their requirements?

- How have their requirements changed over time?

If you do not get a robust answer to these questions, that leader has an opportunity to strengthen their understanding of their stakeholders.

- **a--What No Leader Can Delegate at Any Level:**

  Leaders can have help determining their stakeholder requirements (□), but when that is done, every leader must (a) **understand their stakeholder requirements.**

  If the leader does not understand their Stakeholder Requirements, they are not qualified to lead the organization!

Be Careful!

Customers may or may not tell you what will truly drive their decisions and resulting actions. Considering the following conditions:

Customer (and possibly all stakeholder) **Requirements:**

What The Customer:	Knows	Doesn't Know
Tells You	Quadrant 1 Where We Document Their 'Requirements'	Quadrant 2
Doesn't Tell You	Quadrant 3	Quadrant 4

Quadrant 1: This is where most organizations get their customer requirements.

In fact, if you accept that your listening isn't perfect, you get their requirements from a subset of this quadrant. It's frustrating for customers when it is obvious the person or organization providing products or services doesn't listen effectively enough to understand what has been clearly stated by the customer.

We have all been in the situation where we state our requirements clearly and they are not heard or understood. All too often the supplier hears 'what the average customer wants' and not what you told them.

The lesson to leaders is: It is not enough to go through the motions of listening – you must really understand what the customer is telling you.

Question: Does the leader understand the stakeholder's requirements well enough that, if they repeat them to the stakeholder, the stakeholder agrees they are accurate?

Quadrant 2: These are requirements which are either:

- Invalid because they are not really needed and are less important than Quadrant 1.

- Invalid because they may be stated by the customer but are not possible or not economically feasible.

- Invalid because they will not drive the customer's final purchase decision, and certainly will not drive their loyalty.

Quadrant 3: These are requirements which may be genuine, but our customer research isn't sophisticated enough to gather these from the customer. This is particularly dangerous for a leader because the customer knows the requirements and the leader does not.

Question: How well do we know the customer's environment, and what their requirements "should be?"

The obvious insight here is that our ability to understand the customer's environment may help the customer to establish requirements which are truly important to them in how they use our product or service.

Quadrant 4: These are requirements which may be valuable to the customer, but the customer has never thought about them. NOTE: This is the Quadrant which many of Apple's products come from. The customer did not ask for them, but once they see them, they become valuable to the customer.

"You can't just ask customers what they want, and then try to give it to them. By the time you get it built, they'll want something new."
Steve Jobs

What is a Satisfied Customer/Stakeholder?

See the definition for Customer Engagement in the Glossary.

When our customer requirements only come from a subset of Quadrant 1, above, how can we expect the customer experience to drive true customer engagement?

Researching customer experience and what is reported as *extremely satisfied* customers can be classified as two distinct groups:

- Rationally satisfied:

    o   Rationally satisfied customers showed no difference in spending characteristics when compared with the unsatisfied ones.

- Emotionally satisfied:

    o   Emotionally satisfied customers are those who are rationally satisfied as well as emotionally attached.
    o   Studies have found that only those emotionally satisfied customers demonstrated brand affinity.

If you're unsatisfied or satisfied but only rationally satisfied, you're going to buy from whoever presents an offering to you that seems logical. But if you're emotionally attached because you're emotionally satisfied, you're always going to do business with the brand that you're emotionally attached to.

The Servant Leader

There are hundreds (thousands?) of passages written on the servant leader. From this book it should be clear that one of your key stakeholders is your workforce.

One of our favorite passages on being a servant leader is the poem "The Bridge."

"The Bridge"
An old man going a lone highway,
came in the evening cold and gray,
to a chasm vast, both deep and wide.
The old man crossed in the twilight dim,
the swollen stream was as naught to him.
But he stopped when safe on the further side,
and built a bridge to span the tide.
"Old man", said a fellow pilgrim near,
"you are wasting your strength in labor here.
Your journey will end with the closing day.
You never again will pass this way.
You've crossed the chasm deep and wide.
Why build this bridge at eventide?"
The laborer lifted his old gray head.
"Good friend, in the path I come," he said.
"There follows after me today

a youth whose feet must pass this way.
This chasm which has been as naught to me,
to that young man may pitfall be.
He too must cross in the twilight dim.
Good friend, I am building this bridge for him. "
Author Unknown

The systematic processes you put in place (including a systematic process to lead) are the bridges that those who follow you will cross.

They will be ambassadors you send forth to a time you won't see.

War Stories from the Road – Skin in the game

Walt: Bob DeRhodes, one of my, great heroes, and maybe greatest of all times at the CIO role, was at Home Depot working for Bob Nardelli. He had a huge project that had a hundred-million-dollar budget. And he and his team couldn't get the EVP that was the owner of that project to show up for the meetings to do the requirements gathering. And so, he went to Nardelli, Bob did, he went to his boss and said, "Look, I can't get this guy to show up for the meetings. We're just going to cancel this project, and we'll move those $100 million dollars into some other areas where we desperately need some energy, and some money." Nardelli says, "Well, are you going to tell him, or do you want me to tell him?" And the hint was that Bob needed to go tell the guy himself. So, Bob goes down the hall, tells the EVP, "Hey, you're not showing up for these project meetings, and you're not even responding to the request. I told the CEO we should cancel your project."

And he said, "You did what? You can't cancel that project." He got all upset and the next thing you know, he's assigned a VP to permanently go to all of the meetings. He's got a VP from his team, and he's dedicated staff. He pulled around thirty people and said, "Okay, you guys are going to go be the subject matter experts. You're going to work with Bob DeRhodes' team, and we're going to build this system for how we manage contractors at the stores." So, Bob says, I didn't know it at the time, but this project was going to cost me my job. But I told my guys, "Yeah, he's got a dedicated team with a VP at the top."

They're dedicated. Let's go ahead and build this thing." He says, "Remember it's a $100 million program." Here's the end of the story, right? And so, we get all through this development of requirements. We build out the solution. We go to the first pilot Home Depot to roll out the solution. And the people there look at us like we've grown seven heads out of our neck. What in the heck have you built? Because this has absolutely nothing to do with what we do here at the store and how we've been managing these contractors.

For people that don't want to do it themselves, they want a contractor resource to come in and do it for them. We want to be able to provide that linkage, but this has nothing to do with what we're doing here. Bob DeRhodes says from stage, he said, "I go sniffing around and I find out, that VP that was the dedicated resource, had never worked in that part of the Home Depot operation. And not ever once had he gone out and talked to anybody at the store level about what those processes were." Those 30 people that were dedicated were pulled randomly from the big guy's team because they were the most available and had the most slack in their schedules.

John: Which means they were not needed.

Walt: And they were not subject matter experts in any part of this process. So, they made up the requirements. They literally did what any guy at a bar will do if you sit down and ask the guy next to you at the barstool, how do you make a million dollars in a month? A lot of times the guy next to you, the drunk next to you at the bar will tell you how to make a million dollars in a month. Now you need to be smart enough to ask the question, have you ever made a million dollars in a month? But the truth is most anybody will make up a story about how he could do it.

In essence, that's what these Home Depot people did. And Bob said, "We wound up losing on this build. We spent all the time and resources to build what these 30 people plus the VP had designed for us. And it had nothing to do with the reality of the store."

❷

SET DIRECTION: The world is a multi-stakeholder environment. Rarely do we do anything that involves only one stakeholder.

In setting direction, every leader must consider all stakeholders' requirements in setting the direction for the group they lead, AND clearly prioritize those requirements. This is called Balancing Requirements.

All stakeholders are not equal, and all stakeholder requirements are not equal. There are plenty of examples where leaders give preference to one set of requirements over others. When a leader does this, they should have a rational reason for their decisions. This is a key role of leaders.

Your direction must align with the VMV of the organization, and you must be the role model for those, including your behavior.

- **b--What No Leader Can Delegate at Any Level:**

  Every leader must **communicate effectively and** have a process to validate that what you think you have communicated is clearly understood by the team.

  It is common for leaders to be confident that they have communicated clearly and are surprised when others do not understand the same message the leader thinks they have communicated.

Several tests for communication effectiveness are documented earlier in this book.

ORGANIZE, PLAN & ALIGN: Every leader must Organize, Plan & Align the work in their group. This requires knowledge of the work to be accomplished, and knowledge of the skills in the workforce.

Annual, monthly, weekly, or daily (depending on your products and services) planning must be performed (as needed by your group), and it needs to include the groups you integrate your products or services with, both inside and outside your organization.

All the work the group is expected to accomplish needs to be assigned. It must be delegated to those who have the capability to be successful, and the workload needs to be fairly spread across the team. It's not enough to communicate to your own satisfaction (b)–every leader must validate that what they have communicated is understood.

Measurement of progress should use both leading and lagging indicators which should be clearly defined and assigned during planning.

Leaders should ensure that, in conjunction with planning the products and services, all the resources needed are available, and the providers of those resources are as clear on the plan, timing, and their requirements, as you are.

Most plans, which advance the performance of the group, include some element of training/developing better skills. If not, the group may not be able to achieve anything they didn't achieve during the previous planning cycle.

Finally, most organizations typically reserve the term "Succession Planning' for the top leaders of the organization. For each leader or group, however, you need to consider:

1. What is the division of skills among the people who report to you?

2. Who is in charge when the leader is out?

3. What is the working relationship between the remaining leaders?

4. Who could ultimately take over the group if the leader leaves on vacation or permanently?

In industry it is common to assume that only the top leaders need to be in the "Succession Plan." This is rarely the case. Think about who has unique skills that would be difficult to replace quickly. For example, if only one person knows how to keep the boiler running, which heats the building, think about what you would do if they were not available.

- ## c--What No Leader Can Delegate at Any Level:

Leaders are required to **validate understanding** of their communication. It is a fatal flaw in a leader's approach to assume everyone on their team fully understands their communication of direction. When there are two or more people involved the chance for miscommunication is there.

IT IS FREQUENTLY A HUGE SURPRISE TO LEADERS THAT THEIR TEAM DID NOT HEAR (OR UNDERSTAND) WHAT THEY ARE CONFIDENT THEY COMMUNICATED CLEARLY. ONE OF THE TECHNIQUES WE RECOMMEND IS AT THE CLOSE OF A MEETING, THE LEADER DOESN'T JUST WALK OUT.

THE LEADER SHOULD ASK ONE OF THE PARTICIPANTS IN THE MEETING TO SUMMARIZE WHAT WAS AGREED—DON'T ASSUME THEY UNDERSTOOD WHAT YOU THOUGHT WAS COMMUNICATED CLEARLY.

ONE LEADER WHO DID THIS EXCLAIMED "WERE WE EVEN AT THE SAME MEETING?"

CHECK WITH THE PEOPLE ON YOUR TEAM TO MAKE SURE YOUR COMMUNICATION IS CLEAR.

ASK THEM TO SAY WHAT THEY UNDERSTAND IS:

- THE GOAL OF THE TEAM
- THEIR GOAL
- WHO THEY SUPPORT
- WHO SUPPORTS THEM

DEPLOY: Deployment must include the alignment of resources.

If the leader has not reconnected with the stakeholders (since step 1) before this step, it needs to be done again. Each of the stakeholders has a role in performing the work or is a recipient of the product or service, and they will evaluate your success. Do they even still want the same thing now?

Work needs to be deployed in a way people understand WHY, HOW, and WHEN, and believe that the work can be accomplished with the given resources. This helps to motivate the stakeholders and build buy-in to success.

- **d--What No Leader Can Delegate at Any Level:**

    Every leader must **inspire success.** If their team members have any why/how/when doubts they must be convinced that the work is important (why), that they have the resources (how), and it is within their ability to finish effectively (when).

    This role often takes on the aspect of understanding the motivation and needs of their team.

    As stated earlier, if the workforce does not think the leader cares about them, why should they follow that leader?

PERFORM: Execute quality work--Leaders must ensure that their organization performs the job they are assigned at the quality level expected.

There is little that is less effective than a leader who assigns work and never monitors it to ensure the process is going as expected, or that the end product will be as expected.

Simply put, leaders must establish quality standards and ensure they are met. This clearly requires that the leader has leading measures, so they know if the work is on track before it is too late to change.

This must be achieved in a manner which uses the competencies of the organization and team members, and in a manner which respects the organization's VMV's and behaviors.

- **e--What No Leader Can Delegate at Any Level:**

  All leaders must **monitor** performance, and based on the goals and progress, make appropriate **adjustments.**

  o This is a serious flaw in many implementation plans. It isn't enough to monitor progress and not make "course corrections." To do so tells your team that you are all talk and won't enforce the standards you have set.

  o Another communication technique is, during the work, to ask the team to reiterate what they feel is an acceptable outcome.

  o If the team is not where the leader thinks they should be, the leader has the responsibility to:

    - Understand the gap.
    - Understand the "why" the gap exists (this is not to punish those involved but may be key to the actions the leader must take to help close the gap).
    - Work with the team to make the course corrections necessary to achieve the end goal(s).

- Use their authority to remove barriers.
- Motivate the team.

6

MEASURE PERFORMANCE: From the previous steps it should be clear that measuring performance is critical.

Establishing the appropriate measures starts with Stakeholder Requirements at step one and ensuring the level of performance expected by each of the stakeholders are reflected in your direction, performance metrics, alignment of resources, and monitoring work.

Leaders must analyze performance against the metrics, results, and benchmarks they have established.

A key leadership responsibility is to understand what is causing the (favorable or unfavorable) performance and make appropriate course corrections. These adjustments should be focused on making (or outperforming) the organizational goals set in **Organize, Plan & Align** (Step 3), and to achieve the quality goals or schedule goals.

This requires performance meetings (this could be a discussion with your team), and evaluation of performance, and adjusting the plan, actions, resources, in-process dates, or completion dates.

ANY MEASURE, BY ITSELF, IS A BAD MEASURE!

IF ONLY ONE MEASURE IS BEING TRACKED, YOU HAVE NO IDEA WHAT "BEHIND THE SCENES" MEASURES OR PERFORMANCE ARE BEING SACRIFICED.

EXAMPLE: WE SAW AN ORGANIZATION WHICH SET A SINGULAR MEASURE TO ANSWER A CUSTOMER CALL IN NO MORE THAN THREE RINGS. MOST PEOPLE WOULD AGREE THIS IS A LAUDABLE GOAL AND MAKES SENSE.

ONLY ONE DEPARTMENT COULD ACHIEVE THIS LOFTY GOAL, SO WE WENT THERE TO SEE HOW THEY DID IT. SIMPLE! THE PHONE WOULD RING, AND THEY WOULD PICK UP THE RECEIVER AND HANG UP ON THE CUSTOMER. THEY MADE THE GOAL! TRUE STORY!

A SECOND MEASURE COULD HAVE BEEN HOW MANY CUSTOMERS ARE NOT ABLE TO CONNECT WITH THE ORGANIZATION, OR IN THEIR CASE, HOW MANY CUSTOMERS ARE HUNG-UP ON.

One of the most important aspects of measuring performance is to develop "leading" measures (see the description below). These are criteria which you can monitor to understand whether you are on track to meet the final goals. This is tough to do for many leaders but is critical.

We've often said, "If you want to see an adult sweat, give them their organizational goals (usually predominately outcome or lagging measures) and ask them what the leading measures are to drive those outcomes." Nevertheless, without leading measures, all work tracking is like walking toward a cliff– "so far, so good," until it's too late.

- **f--What No Leader Can Delegate at Any Level:**

    A critical aspect of measuring performance is to **identify high performance.**

Unless the high performing individuals, teams or groups are identified, you as a leader don't really care about the goals, measures, or impacts.

One of the quickest ways a leader can destroy performance is to recognize the wrong individual, team, or group. Everyone knows who the performers are—but does the leader know?

The leadership system says you shouldn't have as your first concern, "I wonder if Alan's working hard today. I wonder--he doesn't seem to be working that hard."

Your concerns should be:

o   Does Alan understand the organization's objectives?
o   Does he understand his objectives?
o   Does he understand the impact of his objectives on the organization's objectives?

Because if he doesn't understand those things, it doesn't make any difference if he's working hard.

Consider this perspective: The metrics you focus on should be either:

•   **Required** (higher authority, either in the company or from other organizations who have authority over you.)

Or

- **Actionable** You need the metric to track your performance or progress against a goal.

If it's not one of these two drivers, why do you need the measure? It's not required, and you cannot use it!

There is a big difference between tracking performance (lagging) and driving performance (leading).

In planning, and particularly Strategic Planning, leaders are always anxious to get to the right Strategic Objectives. We've seen leaders which have that as their key focus. Our experience, however, is there are a few things which must be understood before you can get to "the right" Strategic Objectives.

Baldrige has taught the following flow-down hierarchy:

CRITICAL: Understanding the following flow and linkage makes it easier to determine our objectives.

- **Strategic Challenges:** Understanding what is coming at us from the outside we do not control

- **Success Factors:** Understanding what anybody in our business needs to excel at

- **Strategic Advantages:** Understanding our organization's strengths vs. the competitor's

- **Strategic Opportunities:** Understanding what is happening in the marketplace (or internally) which is an opportunity the organization can leverage.

- **Strategic Objectives:** Understanding what we will be stronger in once our objectives are achieved.

Once the Strategic Objectives are defined, they must be deployed down the organization to each individual (or team), so their activities and goals are linked to the overall organizational objectives.

Leaders must always know where the performance of the organization is (using both leading and lagging indicators). In addition, they must clearly see the plan to be better and to achieve the goals and objectives.

Most organizations use 90+% lagging indicators.

If you want to conduct a productive team exercise, give them their measures (most, if not all, are lagging) and ask them to go to the flip chart and document the leading indicators that drive their lagging measures. They typically struggle to identify them. When this is then discussed with the entire leadership team, the entire team can struggle with this.

Leading indicators allow you to drive change; lagging indicators help you measure the effectiveness of programs. All indicators should be combined and reviewed multiple times annually.

Think about your metrics in the following context:

Metrics	Leading Indicators	Lagging Indicators
"Run" The Business	~ 1%	90+%
"Change" The Business	~ 1%	~ 5%

Sadly, the vast majority of indicators tracked by most organizations (90+%?), will also be "Run" the business lagging indicators.

It's not easy to develop the appropriate measures in the other 3 quadrants, but it must be done. You will never have 25% of your metrics in each quadrant, but there should be meaningful ones in each quadrant.

To develop these, start with a discussion with your team.

- Start with who your stakeholders are (all your stakeholders), and what they expect from you and your organization.

- A key aspect of that discussion, however, is to ensure the discussion does not fall into the old paradigm of, "Any measure not achieved has negative consequences." If that's the atmosphere, the discussion will be limited in scope and effectiveness.

When we present the Leadership System, you will plainly see that the metrics must start (and end) with the requirements and needs of your stakeholders. Each stakeholder in a particular group may not have the same requirements as the others in their group.

YEARS AGO, WE WORKED WITH A COMPANY WHO MANUFACTURED LIGHT BULBS—ONE PRODUCT, AND FAIRLY STRAIGHTFORWARD.

THEY HAD FIVE KEY CUSTOMERS, AND ALL FIVE HAD THE SAME NEEDS.

HOWEVER, EACH OF THE CUSTOMERS HAD THOSE REQUIREMENTS IN A DIFFERENT ORDER OF PRIORITY.

IF YOU DID NOT UNDERSTAND THE PRIORITY FOR EACH CUSTOMER, YOU DID NOT UNDERSTAND THE CUSTOMER.

SAME PRODUCT, SAME REQUIREMENTS, BUT A DIFFERENT SEQUENCE OF REQUIREMENTS.

REWARD & RECOGNIZE: Once a leader knows the high performers (Step f above) it's key that the high-performance group or person be recognized.

This can be as simple as verbal or a written acknowledgement, or as formal as using the organization's performance evaluation system with a salary or bonus incentive.

- **g--What No Leader Can Delegate at Any Level:**

  Reward and recognition should include **a celebration** which is **motivating**. A key aspect of this is to understand what the individual, team, or group being recognized values.

If the person has 10 certificates, they may not be motivated by another one.

On an assessment, I talked to a lady who had a dozen certificates in her cubicle. When asked what they were for, her reply was "I have no idea." It didn't leave us with the impression that another certificate was going to improve job satisfaction, motivation, or job performance.

Some research has shown that what is frequently important to the workforce (in general terms):

o   From the middle of the organization down:

-   *"Was the recognition given to me in front of my peers?"* A Warning Side Note: Not all employees have the same desire for public recognition. What is motivating to one can almost be considered "punishment" by another (more private or reserved) person. It is key for the leader to know how your efforts to recognize them will be viewed.

o   From the middle of the organization up:

-   *"Who gave me the recognition? Was it the top leader?"*

What some organizations have done is to learn what is unique to the individuals, teams, or groups and what they would find motivating. This knowledge even goes back to understanding stakeholder requirements.

If you give someone recognition in a form which is important to them, it carries a lot of weight.

GOOD EXAMPLE: WE VISITED AN ORGANIZATION WHERE ONE PERSON WAS RECOGNIZED FOR HIGH PERFORMANCE. THAT INDIVIDUAL WAS DESERVING, AND EVERYONE KNEW IT.

THEY PAID FOR HIM TO GO TO A REUNION HE COULD NOT AFFORD TO ATTEND, BUT HIGHLY DESIRED.

MANY OF THE PEOPLE WE INTERVIEWED MENTIONED THIS AND WERE PROUD THAT THE COMPANY WAS CARING ENOUGH TO GIVE A FORM OF RECOGNITION WHICH WAS HIGHLY VALUED.

NOT A GOOD EXAMPLE: WE VISITED ANOTHER ORGANIZATION WHERE ONE PERSON WAS RECOGNIZED AS "EMPLOYEE OF THE YEAR" THE PREVIOUS YEAR. WHEN WE WERE TALKING TO HER INDIVIDUALLY AND CONGRATULATED HER FOR SUCH A PRESTIGIOUS ACCOMPLISHMENT, WE WERE ABSOLUTELY DUMBFOUNDED WHEN SHE SAID, "YES, BUT DON'T TELL ANYONE, THE OTHERS ARE NOT SUPPOSED TO KNOW THIS!" SHE HAD SOME LEVEL OF FEAR THAT HER COWORKERS WOULD FIND OUT ABOUT HER RECOGNITION. SAD.

IMPROVE: Leaders are the role model for everything that happens in an organization.

A phrase we always listen for from the workforce, and especially from leaders is, "aren't we good already." There is very little more devastating than this attitude. It normally conveys:

- Satisfaction with the status quo

- Not enough humility or self-reflection

- No desire to work hard to improve further

- Typically, no systematic process for improvement, which everybody is trained in and expected to use

- No path for improvement, which will yield a higher-performing organization in the future

- No path of improvement, which will keep the organization competitive

In seconds the entire organization knows that all the talk about improvement is window dressing, and the boss doesn't really mean it.

It should be clear by now that leaders should insist that a systematic improvement approach is used, everybody is trained, everybody is expected to improve, and improvement must be process based.

When there is a problem, and the leader asks, "Who," they have already lost! They should ask, "Where did the process go wrong?" NOT, "Who was to blame?"

IN THE PAST I (JOHN) WOULD SPEND ABOUT A WEEK EACH YEAR GOING THROUGH FACTORIES WITH A JAPANESE PROFESSOR, WHO WAS ON THE DEMING AWARD COMMITTEE (ONE OF JAPAN'S HIGHEST AWARDS FOR EXCELLENCE).

ONE YEAR IN A FACTORY WE SAW THAT A FORK-TRUCK HAD CUT THE CORNER TOO SHARP AND HIT THE PRODUCT.

THE FORK-TRUCK DRIVER EVEN SAW US LOOKING AT THE DAMAGE AND TOLD US, "YEAH, I HIT THAT THIS MORNING."

HAVING GROWN UP IN FACTORIES, THE NORMAL RESPONSE IS TO FUSS AT THE FORK-TRUCK DRIVER (WHICH ACCOMPLISHES NOTHING). AT BEST THAT ONLY DEALS WITH A SYMPTOM, AND NOT A ROOT-CAUSE.

SINCE IT WAS LATE IN THE DAY, LATE IN THE WEEK, AND I WAS TIRED, I ASKED A QUESTION WHICH WAS AIMED AT SIMPLE HUMOR. "PROFESSOR, WHAT COULD POSSIBLY DAMAGE PRODUCT THIS WAY?"

I WILL NEVER FORGET HIS ANSWER: "I HAVE NO IDEA; WE HAVE NO DATA!"

SURE, THE DRIVER HIT THE PRODUCT, BUT FUSSING AT THE DRIVER WAS DEALING WITH A SYMPTOM AND NOT THE ROOT CAUSE.

THERE COULD BE A NUMBER OF ROOT CAUSES:

- TRAINING
- STORAGE
- SCHEDULING
- EQUIPMENT
- AND MANY OTHERS

IF YOU DON'T FIX THE ROOT CAUSE, YOU DON'T FIX THE PROBLEM.

The tightrope all leaders must walk is between recognizing high performance and being passionate about improvement.

- You don't want your drive for improvement to be demotivating to the high achievers.

- You also don't want the workforce to be afraid of identifying problems. Problems in an organization rarely get better as time passes.

Where to improve goes all the way back to stakeholder requirements.

What are the pressures leaders have for improvement?

- Customers want more value

- Stockholders want more return

- Competitors want more of your market share

- Regulators want more conformity

- Employees want more empowerment

- Suppliers want more consistency of orders

And the list could go on. Every stakeholder (and competitor) wants something.

As a leader do you understand these pressures, and are you improving in each area?

After Action Review (AAR)

One of the things the military does exceedingly well is an AAR. After each major event they meticulously go over what went well and what can be improved.

In the corporate world, however, this discussion is not frequently held, and constructive comments can easily be viewed as negative, or worse accusatory.

Leaders must fight against this attitude and listen to all comments, even if they include insights into their own actions or decisions, or how they were interpreted.

The "Lessons Learned" during an AAR must be shared, at a minimum, with everybody who can use them to improve.

Corrective actions can include plans, resources, training, teamwork and almost every aspect of team performance.

"You've got your passion, you've got your pride,
but don't you know that only fools are satisfied."
Billy Joel
Song: "Vienna"

This is another point where a leader needs to reconnect with the stakeholders, especially customers. Where the stakeholders recognize performance, the leader needs to pass it on to the appropriate group or person, since this can be a genuine source of pride and motivation.

Our experience shows that it is critical that the organization adopts a systematic method of solving problems. A brief online search for Systematic Problem Solving showed 2,440,000 results.

You don't need a dozen approaches. One that everybody knows and uses throughout the organization is much better. It develops a common language and purpose.

ONE OF THE COMMON QUESTIONS WE USE IN HIRING INTERVIEWS IS TO ASK THE PERSON TO DESCRIBE THE LAST (OR A LARGE) MISTAKE THEY MADE.

IF THEY CANNOT DO THIS, THEY EITHER ARE:

- NOT BEING HONEST WITH YOU
- HAVEN'T DONE ANYTHING OF SIGNIFICANCE.
- DID NOT LEARN FROM THE EXPERIENCE OR DID NOT LEARN HOW NOT TO MAKE THE SAME MISTAKE AGAIN.

IT'S SIGNIFICANT IF THEY SMILE, DIVE INTO AN EXAMPLE, AND HAVE A CLEAR AAR AND IMPROVEMENT PROCESS. THEN THEY CAN EXPLAIN THE LEARNING PROCESS AND HOW THEY WILL DO THINGS DIFFERENTLY.

IN ADDITION, IT CAN BE AN INDICATION OF THE ATTITUDE THEY WILL BRING WITH THEM TO YOUR ORGANIZATION IF THEY ARE HIRED.

DO THEY LOOK AT PROBLEM SOLUTIONS IN TERMS OF "WHO" (A PERSON OR TEAM), OR DO THEY LOOK FOR "WHAT" (A PROCESS OR SET OF CIRCUMSTANCES)?

Frequently we will ask an organization to list their problem-solving approaches and:

- How many people were trained in each approach?

- When were they trained?

- How do you keep the knowledge current?

- How do you track the results from using each approach?

- What have been the performance improvement results for each approach in the last year?

- Does your accounting department agree with the "savings" or other improvements claimed?

RETURNING FROM LUNCH AT A HIGH PERFORMING ORGANIZATION THE SENIOR VICE PRESIDENT OF MARKETING ASKED US, "DID WE GET ANY STARS IDEAS (WHAT THEY CALLED THEIR IMPROVEMENTS) FROM OUR DISCUSSION AT LUNCH? I STILL NEED THREE MORE THIS YEAR."

THIS MADE IT CLEAR THAT EVERYBODY NEEDED TO GENERATE IMPROVEMENT IDEAS, EVEN THE SENIOR EXECUTIVES, AND EVEN THE DISCUSSION AT LUNCH WAS MINED FOR IMPROVEMENT IDEAS!

WHEN HIS BOSS (THE CEO) OF THAT ORGANIZATION WAS ASKED IN AN EMPLOYEE MEETING ABOUT THE REQUIREMENT FOR A CERTAIN NUMBER OF IDEAS FROM EACH EMPLOYEE EVERY YEAR, HE REPLIED, "I AGREE WITH YOU. I DID NOT AGREE WITH WHAT THE SENIOR LEADERS DID. I WANTED TO FIRE THE PERSON, BUT THE SENIOR LEADERS TALKED ME OUT OF IT."

AS CRUDELY PUT AS THIS ANSWER WAS:

1. THERE WAS NO DOUBT WHERE THE CEO STOOD.
2. THERE WAS NO DOUBT ON HIS PASSION FOR IMPROVEMENT FOR EVERYONE (HIMSELF INCLUDED); AND
3. THERE WERE NO MORE QUESTIONS ABOUT THIS CULTURAL REQUIREMENT-- EVER.

It's sad to see a scattering of improvement approaches, not kept current, not used, no real documented improvement. If that is the case, you have just wasted time and money in training, and everybody knows it.

Once an organization adopts the culture of improvement it is impressive to watch what can happen. If the organization has a 5% profit margin, a dollar saved by an improvement can have the same impact of 20 dollars in new organizational revenue.

- **h--What No Leader Can Delegate at Any Level:**

  Continuous Improvement needs to be systematic. Systematic tools should be taught, and importantly, leaders should insist they are used and track the progress for every person and group.

  What Doesn't Work: Tragically some organizations use Performance Excellence or Systematic Problem-solving Training as an "activity" that everybody gets checked off on, and not as a way to change the culture and the effectiveness of the organization.

  It's not unusual in those organizations to see everybody trained in something they never use. Once again, that is simply a waste of time and money, and a subliminal inditement on the leader's authenticity.

Deploying a Leadership System

We have discovered (the hard way) that once you have developed a Leadership System it needs to be deployed down to every leader.

If every leader in the organization has been "briefed" on the Leadership System (even if it is by their direct boss in a 100% comprehensive flow-down)–the organization thinks it is 100% deployed, but there is absolutely NO traction.

It simply was a *spectator sport* even though everybody was involved in the flow-down.

WHAT DOES WORK--Is for each leader to document how *they* will do steps 1 through 8 and Steps a through h, and what they have documented is discussed with their direct supervisor. This becomes real, memorable, and is the genesis of conversations that probably would not happen any other way.

It is no longer a *spectator sport*; it just became a *contact sport*.

This can be done using a workbook with the information above, and space for the leader to write in what they will do to achieve each step. Then the discussion with their direct supervisor can be productive in showing the leader where they need to improve and how to improve.

This is never "once and done," but can be something a leader uses on a continual basis, and these reviews become a part of the culture.

Think about the use of a personal workbook.

As with all "gifts" some leaders will use it, and some will not. The leader with a passion and humility will have a workbook which is dog-eared in a few years through use and documenting their personal improvements in their approach to each step.

It also can become a point of discussion between leaders who are peers, where they learn from each other.

The initial benefits of this approach are manifold, but include:

- A meaningful conversation between each leader and their direct supervisor

- A consensus of how the leader is doing on each step

- Ideas of how their performance can be improved, without the impact of being a short-term performance evaluation

- Ideas on who does well at key steps which need to be improved, and possibly those who could help the leader

- Training required

- New metrics required

- Other help required

SUMMARIZING LEADERSHIP RESPONSIBILITIES USING A LEADERSHIP SYSTEM

Every leader must ensure that their organization effectively addresses each of the items in the boxes on the Leadership System:

1. Stakeholders

2. Set Direction

3. Organize, Plan & Align

4. Deploy

5. Perform

6. Measure Performance

7. Reward and Recognize

8. Improve

A leader can have help with these, but when the step is completed, they must validate the work's output, so the organization knows what the leader stands for, endorses, and expects.

The connecting behaviors on the Leadership System are:

a. Understand Stakeholder Requirements

b. Communicate Effectively

c. Validate Understanding

d. Inspire Success

e. Monitor & Adjust

f. Identify High Performance

g. Celebrate & Motivate

h. Continuous Improvement

No leader can delegate these behaviors at any level of the organization. Leaders must act in this manner to be a role model for their direct reports, as well as for the rest of the organization.

The Result

Internally

- Your workforce now has a consistent approach to leading and a common bond to help each other in what is required from each leader.

Externally

- Every organization competes for the best talent in the marketplace.

This argument will not have the same appeal to all candidates, but you would now be qualified to say: "Lots of organizations may wish to hire you--But we can teach you to lead. That is a skill which will last your lifetime!

 Chapter 7 Keys:

Chapter 7: A Mature Leadership System

- The source provides an example of a mature leadership system used by Prince William Water.

- Leaders must engage with stakeholders to understand their requirements.

- Leaders must balance stakeholder requirements when setting direction.

- Succession planning is important for leaders at all levels, not just the top.

- Leaders must ensure clear communication and validate understanding.

- Deployment of plans must include the alignment of resources.

- Leaders must monitor and adjust plans to achieve goals.

- Leaders must use both leading and lagging indicators when measuring performance.

- Leaders must identify high performance.

- Leaders must reward and recognize high performance.

- Leaders must conduct after-action reviews to identify lessons learned.

- Leaders must use a consistent problem-solving approach.

- Leaders should use a personal workbook to document their leadership system and track their progress.

SECTION 4

Improving Your Leadership

8

The Reality of a Strong Leader

Reality is the stewarded domain of the leader. REALITY is the responsibility of the leader. The leader is on a constant and never-ending quest to understand and convey what is real and to navigate the dynamic nature of reality--it changes all the time! How does a leader meet this responsibility?

Both of us have been fans of Colin Powell's Rules of Leadership for many years. General Powell's framing of reality in his rules is the most important aspect. Get into reality, stay there as long as you're able and adjust to it in a way that empowers you and your teams.

In the next two illustrations you'll see General Powell's Rules–13 simple approaches to "keeping it real" and you'll see a grab from social media that reflects the ultimate truth of being a leader: You need to know and understand what is happening.

Colin Powell's Thirteen Rules of Leadership

1. It ain't as bad as you think. It will look better in the morning.

2. Get mad, then get over it.

3. Avoid having your ego so close to your position that when your position falls, your ego goes with it.

4. It can be done.

5. Be careful what you choose. You may get it.

6. Don't let adverse facts stand in the way of a good decision.

7. You can't make someone else's choices. You shouldn't let someone else make yours.

8. Check small things.

9. Share credit.

10. Remain calm. Be kind.

11. Have a vision. Be demanding.

12. Don't take counsel of your fears or naysayers.

13. Perpetual optimism is a force multiplier.

Listening Skills

We have five senses given to us at birth in the base package. Some leaders have a sixth sense and are somewhat more intuitive or psychic than those with just sight, taste, touch, smell, and hearing abilities.

The ability to hear may be at the top of the leader's reality-sensing skills. Listening when people are bringing you problems, challenges, or issues is the easiest thing to do if you can check your ego and concentrate on the nature of the thing being discussed.

THE DIAGNOSIS

After my colleague John Mamer stepped down as dean of the UCLA Anderson School of Management, he wanted to take a stab at teaching strategy. To acquaint himself with the subject, he sat in on ten of my class sessions. Somewhere around class number seven we were chatting about pedagogy and I noted that many of the lessons learned in a strategy course come in the form of the questions asked as study assignments and asked in class. These questions distill decades of experience about useful things to think about in exploring complex situations. John gave me a sidelong look and said, "It looks to me as if there is really only one question you are asking in each case. That question is 'What's going on here?' "

John's comment was something I had never heard said explicitly, but it was instantly and obviously correct. A great deal of strategy work is trying to figure out what is going on. Not just deciding what to do, but the more fundamental problem of comprehending the situation.

In most organizations, you will hear of the problem long before you're able to see it, taste it, touch it, smell it or see it. Your customers or your people will TELL you about it. Richard Rumelt describes this scenario in his book *Good Strategy/Bad Strategy*:

Listening intently means listening with the intention of really hearing and understanding what they are telling you.

This is not easy.

George Bernard Shaw said, "The worst part of communication is the illusion that it actually happened."

Years ago, I (John) was in a senior position in a large company. Each year we would get a sealed envelope from the CEO's office telling us the new salary package. So how did I find out? The week before we would hear from the shop floor, and they were never wrong!

They knew the people who emptied the trash cans at corporate!

Questioning Skills

Just because you listened and nodded, doesn't mean that you heard and understood.

How can you make sure that you hear and understand?

Use active listening skills like paraphrasing--put what they are telling you in your own words and share that with them. Check and see if it lines up with what and how they are telling the tale.

Many times, you find that you must go through this exercise multiple times to finally arrive at an agreement that YOU have heard them. Oftentimes, because the leader is 'above' the problem sharer in the organization chart, the "lower" person assumes too quickly that you have heard AND understood. This premature assumption of understanding has bitten a lot of teams in the rear over the years. Therefore, it is your responsibility to make sure that YOU (the leader) really understand the issue before you lose access to the sharer. Again, REALITY is the domain of the leader.

What else can you do to make sure that you really understand? What other skill set does a leader use to get to the scope, the impact area, the potential damage, the constraints on possible solutions?

Questions!

Exactly, you use your questioning skills and ask lots of questions.

Note: You MUST establish an environment where questioning is viewed as being engaged and interested and grateful for the information. You cannot allow an environment (and we have been a part of this culture) where all questions by leaders are viewed as being critical or unsupportive.

You ask leading questions. You ask open-ended questions. You prompt for more details by saying, "Tell me more about that." You reflect your understanding of the answers and seek confirmation or validation of your understanding throughout the process. You thank the speaker and show your gratitude.

Question To Learn and not to Criticize

You ask questions about the problem, challenge, or issue in a way that is not attacking the messenger, and either intentionally or unintentionally making them feel foolish or disrespected for bringing this to your attention.

Your goal is to get to reality, not to twist it by focusing on the wrong things. Any hint of criticism in your approach to asking questions will inevitably turn the questioning into an interrogation or inquisition (both are bad) and will result in the sharer becoming more closed or guarded--the opposite of what you need to get a clear idea of what is going on.

The harder you make it on the messengers, the more likely they are to stop bringing you messages.

Communication Skills

Your communication needs to be understood, but it also needs to flow down your organization undistorted.

Humility

A strong or competent leader is almost always humble. Humility is not the absence of an Ego—every human has an Ego (also comes stock in the base package with the five senses).

Humility is an awareness that keeps the Ego in check, and when used this way Humility helps connect to others quickly and effectively and helps clear the way to the openness that lets real truths emerge in the conversation.

In *Good to Great* by Jim Collins, he reported that the thirteen companies in the book were led by what he called "the Level 5 leader" --a person who had their ego in check and cared more about the needs of the company and the people than he or she appeared to care about their own needs.

WHEN TWO LARGE ORGANIZATIONS WERE MERGING AN EMPLOYEE ON THE SHOP FLOOR TOLD US "NOBODY HAS TOLD ME WHAT IS GOING ON WITH THE MERGER, AND I AM RIGHT IN THE MIDDLE OF IT!"

WE WENT TO HIS CEO AND REPORTED THE FINDING. THE CEO SAID HE HAD RECORDED MULTIPLE VIDEOS DESCRIBING THE MERGER, AND THAT WE SHOULD GO TALK TO THE VP OF COMMUNICATIONS.

THE VP OF COMMUNICATIONS SHOWED US 51 VEHICLES OF COMMUNICATION TO EMPLOYEES INCLUDING A PACKAGE SENT TO EVERY EMPLOYEE'S HOME!

- 51 COMMUNICATIONS
- A PACKAGE DESCRIBING THE MERGER SENT TO HIS HOME.
- 5 VIDEOS BY THE CEO

HOW IN THE WORLD COULD THE EMPLOYEE MAKE THIS STATEMENT?

THEN IT DAWNED ON US THAT HIS CONCERN WAS VALID!

WHY: HIS DIRECT BOSS HAD NOT TOLD HIM WHAT HE/SHE THOUGHT WAS HAPPENING, AND HOW IT WOULD DIRECTLY AFFECT HIS JOB!

LESSON LEARNED: THE EMPLOYEE DID NOT KNOW HOW IT WOULD DIRECTLY AFFECT HIM OR HIS WORK, AND COMMUNICATION MUST GO/BE TRANSLATED ALL THE WAY DOWN THE ORGANIZATION REGARDING THE IMPACT.

Humility is essential to leadership because it is the bridge to authenticity and vulnerability in the human-to-human interface. The unchecked ego is a barrier to this connection and prevents both authenticity and vulnerability.

Good Follower

A competent leader is of necessity a good follower. In most organizations leadership roles are distributed across and down into the company. In a sense, everyone is a follower of someone else's leadership.

The CEO is responsible and accountable to the board of directors, shareholders, and ultimately, to the customers and the marketplace.

As a good follower, you too need to bring the same skills and abilities to the table: Listening, Questioning, and Humility are the keys to the win!

100% Commander's Intent

The skills and abilities are critical to your ability to understand what we in the military call "the Commander's Intent" --what is the objective and why does the top-level leader want to accomplish that objective?

In the military, we frequently issue written orders and publish regulations to make it harder for people to misunderstand the Commander's Intent.

Verbal orders sometimes (most of the time) get mistranslated or relayed incorrectly--kind of like the children's game of Telephone. By the time the phrase gets to the end, it's almost invariably something different than what the original was.

Written orders are shareable with little loss in transmission.

REMEMBER THE "WHAT YOU LOST" SECTION? ONE OF THE THINGS YOU MUST DO TO BE A GOOD FOLLOWER IS TO SUPPORT THE TEAM AS SEEN IN THE BOEING OPERATING PRINCIPLES IN THE APPENDIX).

DISAGREEMENT IS HEALTHY AND ENCOURAGED, BUT ONCE A DECISION IS MADE, WE PROACTIVELY SUPPORT IT.

JOHN'S PROUDEST MOMENT AS A LEADER:

IN A KEY LEADERSHIP POSITION THE LEADERSHIP TEAM DISCUSSED A DECISION. I FOUGHT AGAINST THE DECISION AS HARD AS I COULD. I LOST AND THE TEAM DECIDED TO DO IT.

THREE WEEKS LATER, DURING IMPLEMENTATION, ONE OF MY KEY MANAGERS SAID TO ME: "THIS IS EASY FOR YOU, YOU HAVE ALWAYS WANTED TO DO THIS."

THAT WAS ONE OF MY PROUDEST MOMENTS AS A LEADER. IT WASN'T MY IDEA OR PREFERENCE, BUT MY TEAM SAW ME ACT AS IF IT WAS—I WAS PROACTIVELY SUPPORTING THE TEAM'S DECISION.

Prioritizing

Every leader has a set of tasks they need to accomplish in order to advance the mission, achieve the vision, and maintain consistency with the values of the company or team. In a previous job our motto was, "If you had all the resources anybody could do it." How do you do this prioritization?

In his book, *The Seven Habits of Highly Effective People*, Stephen M. R. Covey popularized the Eisenhower Quadrants.

	URGENT	NOT URGENT
IMPORTANT	**Problems** **Panic** Crises Pressing Problems Projects with Deadlines Catastrophes 1	**Prevention** **Planning** Productive activities Preventative activities Relationship building Recognizing new opportunities Planning Recreation 2
NOT IMPORTANT	**Puny** 3 **Pesterments** Interruptions Most email Most phone calls Most meetings Proximate pressing matters Popular activities	4 **Piddling** **Pastimes** Trivia Busy work Most email Most phone calls Time wasters Pleasant activities

In **Quadrant 1,** the tasks are both urgent and important. These could be described as "fighting your fires."

In **Quadrant 3,** the list is urgent but not important. These could be described as "fighting somebody else's fires for them."

In **Quadrant 4,** the list is neither urgent nor important. These are things you should not even spend your time on. These are the phone calls you do not return, the tasks you do not do, and even tasks you do not assign to somebody else. It would waste their time.

We have seen very senior teams who estimate that 45% of their time is spent on Quadrant 4 activities! Think about your own ratio.

Leaders must work on their lists to reduce the size of quadrants 1 and 3 and neutralize entirely quadrant 4.

What about **Quadrant 2**?

In quadrant two, the list of tasks is important but not urgent. This quadrant is what you can delay, but activities in this box may form your entire future!

You can always delay:

- Developing and working on your strategy

- Developing and working on customer relationships

- Developing your workforce

- Improving your communication skills or communication

- Understanding stakeholder needs and wants, etc.

Quadrant 2 is critical **to your future**--If you don't spend adequate time here your future is not being planned, developed, and nurtured. Your future is being ignored and left to random events or chances.

Trust

Trust is the glue which holds the team together, however, most teams never talk about trust.

They will probably be offended because what they heard is, "I don't trust you!"

So--how can we have the glue that keeps us together, and not talk about it?

We use a process where each team member fills out (on their own) the answers to four questions:

1. What do you need to do to earn my trust?

2. What do you need to do to lose my trust?

3. Once trust is lost, what do you need to do to regain my trust?

4. What do you need to do to lose my trust forever?

Once each person finishes their answers, the team breaks up into groups of 2 or 3 and discusses their answers.

Then the entire team comes together and discusses what their breakout sessions found.

The big surprise in this entire exercise is that EVERYONE has a slightly different answer to these questions.

For Example:

- In my own case, I do not have an answer to numbers 3 or 4–we parted company at question 2, but the breach of trust in question 2 must be clear or blatant. If you want to work with me, you must understand my Trust Profile. If you lose my trust, it will not come back.

- I was partnered with a person who didn't have an answer to question 4–you could almost never lose her trust.

Now the team CAN discuss trust.

You are no longer discussing whether you trust each other, you are typically discussing a specific situation, and how each of you viewed that situation given your individual *Trust Profiles.*

If you are going to work closely with someone you need to understand their unique Trust Profile.

Trust Can Be Situational

As counterintuitive as this sounds, consider for a moment that it could be true. To trust someone with something you must be sure they have the integrity, desire, and capability to do what you are asking of them.

You don't want to ask the head of manufacturing to answer the IRS's audit report - - their intention may be honorable, but they may not be the best person on the team to do this or even understand the IRS laws or concerns.

Other Examples of Situational Trust:

- I am honest, and have the very best of intentions, but I am 30 years out of practice in taking care of a newborn. You can trust me to do my best, but I'm pretty rusty on the things I would need to do.

- We were working with a group of fighter pilots and one of them told us, "I trust everyone here with my life and do so every day. We fly in such close formation that I must have 100% trust in their skills. I would not, however, trust anyone here with my wife!"

> *"The supreme quality for leadership is unquestionably integrity. Without it no real success is possible."*
>
> **Dwight D. Eisenhower**

Tuning

One skill that we rarely see in any leadership training, or texts is the skill of tuning your organization. In the spirit of driving, we know that engines need to be tuned. There's a great commercial out right now by Chevy that features a grandfather explaining to his grandson how to listen to the engine and make adjustments to get the timing right.

Imagine that you are a band member playing saxophone in your high school band. You come into the practice area with your instrument out and ready to play. You have your sheet music on the stand in front of you.

The band leader says, "OK everyone, let's all play a concert B-flat and get in tune." So, you all play the note and listen for dissonance. You adjust your instrument until the dissonance is gone and you are in tune with the rest of the band. The more out of tune a group of instruments is from concert B-flat at 440 MHz, the longer this process of tuning takes.

Once the band is at an acceptable level of "tuned" the leader will have the band start to work on the sheet music on the stand. Tuning a "band" is mostly done by ear and feeling much like tuning an organization. If necessary, there are machines that are called "tuners" that can detect the dissonance between a frequency standard (like 440 MHz) and the note being played on an individual instrument. And if everyone's instrument is tuned, then it's safe to assume that the whole band is in tune. After a bit of playing, though, one might

notice a little dissonance creeping in. Over time this increases until, once again, the band leader breaks for another tuning session. When you play your instrument, many times, you lose your "in tune" status and have to re-tune.

In most organizations, getting aligned with the leaders above and below you in the organization chart is difficult. It's hard because of the lack of listening skills, the lack of questioning skills, the lack of humility, and the lack of written, clear orders that allow for easy transmission of the Commander's intent. So, what do you do? You tune, and re-tune your "band" as you "play" together and try to stay aligned to the greatest degree possible.

How do you tune an organization?

- Simple approaches to tuning include beginning meetings with a focus on the purpose of the meeting, and how that purpose aligns with an important strategic objective and why it is important.

  o Years ago, John worked at an organization where someone who called a meeting was required to give you a PAL:

    - **P**–Purpose

- **A**–Agenda
- **L**–Limit (the maximum time the meeting would run)

• Some groups "tune" on safety and start every gathering with a safety briefing.

• Other groups "tur_e" on customer satisfaction and start every gathering with a story of customer engagement and satisfaction.

• Other ways to approach "tuning" are more intensive and intentional such as crafting an incentive plan and awards and recognition programs.

• Building a culture that strives to be in tune and reality-based means thinking about how that works and more importantly, how that works in your unique organiza=ion. This is why every leadership system that we help cl:ents implement is uniquely their own. One size does not fit all when it comes to leadership systems or organizational culture design.

From the high school band, we now move to the high school sports team and down to the individual player to discuss a cultural attribute that we find highly valuable in every organization: The ability to flush the mistake. Study after study of championship caliber players of any and every sport have a refined ability to "flush the mistake." The top coaches from every sport work hard to create a culture in their teams, and in each athlete, that supports and builds on this ability.

Flushing a mistake and moving on to the next play with no baggage (guilt, shame, frustration, anger, etc.) is the hallmark of champions. This is a difference-making ability--those players that do it well perform far better than those who don't. Teams that do this well and help each other with this do far better than those that don't.

How can you apply this in your leadership system? Mistakes are an unavoidable part of learning. Learning is an unavoidable part of innovating and improving. No mistakes--no learning. No learning--no innovation or improvement. Simple. Mistakes are cause for celebration if learning is to happen.

This is a long topic. Some have suggested that mastery requires 10,000 hours or 10,000 attempts. Either seems like a huge investment to me. How do you get the players on your team to invest themselves at this level of commitment?

Learning is the goal; mistakes are the price. Paying the price for learning seems high--sometimes too high--until you consider the price of not learning and staying bad or mediocre at something your team could be good or great at performing. How much does it cost to suck? How much does it cost to compete and lose? Maybe the price of mistakes is not so high after all?

At one company, years ago, I bought a "slushy" in a convenience store that came in a giant cup that said, "Big GULP," on the sides.

I brought the cleaned cup into the shop and decorated it up with glitter and a few branded stickers from our company. For the next three years, the Big Gulp "Trophy" moved from desk to truck to locker to desk to the person who shared their big gulp mistake with the others on the team and had fun learning from each other and getting better and better in each role or job in the group. We celebrated the mistakes and shared the learning. We also got better and better as a team, and we won many awards for excellence over the period. The trophy cost less than five dollars. The learning and sharing were invaluable.

Momentum Shift

While still in a sports mindset, let's talk about the reality of momentum shifts. Even if you are not a huge fan or former player, you no doubt still know about momentum shifts.

We see them best in big team sports like football, baseball, and soccer. They happen in all sports, even one-on-one sports like tennis.

The momentum is going in a particular team's or player's direction and then something happens and the next thing you know, the momentum has shifted, and it is clearly going the other way.

In Atlanta a few years ago, our Falcons had a lead in the Super Bowl over the New England Patriots 28 to 3. The momentum shifted and the Patriots went on to win the game. That was several years ago, but the Atlanta fans are still in shock. Momentum shifts are not only felt on the field but also in the stands and in the hearts and minds of the television or streaming audiences. They happen. They are REAL.

And here is a secret--they can be orchestrated! Sometimes, as a leader, you need to execute a momentum shift for your team. I am not talking about "turnarounds" and "re-foundings" --these take a lot longer and usually require a change in leader and sometimes in players as well.

A momentum shift can be taught and repeated and does not always require a change in leadership to pull off.

What they do require is an unusually high insertion of new energy into the hearts and minds of the team. Just like in sports, momentum shifts usually occur because of a heroic stop when the other team appeared to be unstoppable, or a heroic solo effort that scores against a defense that appeared to be unbreakable.

In a leadership system, you can recognize the need for a momentum shift and use the tools in the system to orchestrate one for your team on demand. As a leader, you can only control what you pay attention to at any given time, and your attitude about whatever that object of attention is in the situation. To make a sudden shift happen for your team, you need to insert a much higher level of energy into the game by increasing the positive energy on your side of the line. We'll talk more about this later.

Time is usually not our friend when we find ourselves about to be defeated on a sports field or in the real-world marketplace. This brings us to another element of reality--the implacable calendar.

Priorities versus Your Calendar

From the earlier discussion of the Eisenhower Urgent/Important Grid, we recognize that we cannot really manage time. Time is also allocated in the base package for all of us and we each get the same 24 hours per day until one-day when we don't, and we move on to the next level of the game.

In the days that you have, you can set and manage your attention and focus. What you give your time and attention to can be important... it can even be noble and inspiring to you and to others. Where you place your attention and focus are your priorities.

Some leaders prioritize badly. You may have worked for one of them in your career. I know I have.

- The worst leaders prioritize external things that are very personal for them but add no value to your organization.

- Some spend all their time and attention putting out fires (Quadrants 1 and 3)--some that are important, but many that aren't important, just urgent and in their face.

- Still others "major in the minors" and spend all their time and focus on being busy, but never seem to move the needle much on getting things done.

- No time (or not enough time) spent in Quadrant 2 is always a mistake and will catch up with you.

As a leader, your organization is counting on you to lead your team to finish the work and get to the value realization for the company for that body of work.

"Plans are nothing... Planning is everything."
Dwight D. Eisenhower

Work-in-progress does not pay the bills. Work successfully delivered on time and within margin gets those bills paid and your salaries and wages as well. As Larry the Cable Guy says, your job is to, "Get 'Er Done!"

At the top of the organization of leaders, the senior-most leaders have a responsibility to align strategic objectives, and to maintain the tuning and alignment throughout the breadth and depth of the organization. Most leaders look at how good they think the strategic objectives are, and don't spend enough time clearly understanding how they are systematically deployed down to every employee. Sometimes this means hearing about things from the lowest level that require re-prioritization.

Sometimes there are external factors like a major competitor going out of business or a new start-up that is taking our market share from us because of better tech or a better approach. In either case, we must adjust and re-prioritize and then communicate that across and down. This is also where having a leadership system can be invaluable.

Agility does not come in a bottle. And you cannot sprinkle it around like fertilizer out of a bag. Agility comes from creating and maintaining a systematic approach to observing, orienting to the new reality, deciding on the best path forward, and then acting on that decision as one.

Agility requires the leader to think about what can/might happen long before it does and think through what your actions would be. This may be the biggest benefit of implementing a leadership system for your team or company.

What we see in those leaders who spend a lot of time in Quadrant 2 planning, is they are aware of the potential scenarios which could unfold, and what they will do if one of those scenarios occurs. Leaders must frequently make "battlefield decisions," and adjust their direction based on reality.

Quadrant 2 is where you focus on taking care of your people.

Legitimate recognition and awards–As discussed in earlier chapters, what you give your attention to and speak about is very telling for your team. As a leader, you are always "on Stage," whether you like it or know it or not. When you give awards and recognize individuals or groups, you are acting out your values by highlighting those people in your organization.

When you do this well, and you are authentic about it, you get more positive performance, and this also serves as a tuning mechanism. When you are not authentic and the suck-ups are getting awards and recognition instead of the individuals or teams that produce the value, you will lose the best and keep the rest.

As a leader you fully control:

- Attitude

- Attention

You get to choose what you pay attention to and choose what your attitude will be toward those things that get your attention. You can even direct yourself to have a cheerful outlook about the opportunities inherent in the biggest problems facing you and your people. If you do not give yourself this direction, your people will see your negative attitude and amplify it for you.

Silver Bullets of Performance

Leaders often ask what are the "silver bullets" that make their job easier and more effective and improve organizational performance. We frequently answer, "there aren't any," and then go on to list a few.

Below are a few techniques which our experience has shown to be a multiplier in the effectiveness of any leader:

- **Walk Around and LISTEN**

The best leaders rarely stay in their office 8 hours a day. They walk through the organization and every employee knows they are both: 1) **Accessible, and 2) Approachable.**

It doesn't any good to know you can talk to the leader if you never see that person (not accessible) or if, when you see them, they do not appear to be approachable.

What is key is what the leader learns from each member of the team. They are not there to talk about themselves or organizational accomplishments, unless it is intended to make the workforce proud of what they have contributed.

 ONE MANUFACTURING VP SHOWED NO TIME ON HIS CALENDAR FOR BEING IN THE FACTORY, TALKING TO THE WORKFORCE, UNDERSTANDING THE PROBLEMS. WHEN CALLED TO TASK FOR THIS HE POINTED OUT A UNIQUELY TITLED "MEETING" WHICH WAS FREQUENTLY ON HIS SCHEDULE. THE "MEETING" HAD A VAGUE TITLE THAT NOBODY COULD TELL WHAT WAS ACTUALLY BEING TALKED ABOUT. HIS SECRETARY KNEW THAT MEETING COULD NEVER BE INTERRUPTED OR SCHEDULED OVER. THAT "MEETING" TIME WAS WHEN HE WAS ACTUALLY OUT ON THE SHOP FLOOR.

 ANOTHER EXAMPLE IS A LEADER WHO WOULD GO TO THE WORK AREA AND LISTEN TO CONCERNS. ONCE HE HEARD THEM, HE WOULD DISCUSS THE ISSUES WITH HIS KEY LEADERSHIP TEAM. HE KNEW IT WAS CRITICAL TO NOT LET THESE DISCUSSIONS BECOME A SESSION WHERE ANYBODY FELT CRITICIZED, BUT WHERE THEY BUILT THE TEAM'S MUTUAL TRUST AS THEY DEVELOPED AN APPROACH TO SOLVING THE PROBLEM.

YEARS AGO, A LEADER WITH A FIFTH-GRADE EDUCATION WAS LEADING A VERY LARGE AIRCRAFT MANUFACTURING ORGANIZATION.

AFTER MONTHS OF SEEING HIM MAKE ENGINEERING, IT, MATERIALS, AND OTHER TECHNICAL DECISIONS ONE OF HIS BRIGHTEST ENGINEERS ASKED HIM, "HOW DO YOU DO THIS EVERY DAY?"

HIS REPLY WAS, "BE HERE AT 5 AM AND I'LL SHOW YOU."

AT 5 HE WAS SITTING ON A SCOOTER AND WENT ENTIRELY THROUGH THE FACTORY. WHAT HE WAS BEING TOLD BY THE LEADERS IN HIS SENIOR MEETINGS WAS NOT THE SAME AS THE STORY HE HEARD IN THE FACTORY AT 5 AM.

In every example, leaders must listen with the ability to truly understand the concept.

- **Post Results**

  o Results and data which is posted tend to improve.

    - Everybody knows what the data are
    - Everybody knows the data are important
    - The "owners" of the data are usually quick to develop a plan to improve the performance.

- **AAA–Acknowledge, Accept, Appreciate**

  o Leaders who acknowledge those who achieve results accept the fact that all learning is not necessarily from success. They appreciate those who achieve, sending a strong message into the organization that it is a team effort, and the leader knows what is happening and why.

- **Leader knows that the problem identified is being worked**

  In high performing organizations there is no attempt to hide bad news. Bad news travels up fast. So... What do leaders do when they get bad news? NOTHING—if it should be worked on by the people involved, and they do not ask for help.

  o Examples of the opposite are:

    - One organization actively hid bad news because every level above them became involved and tried to "help."
    - One organization leader commented, "I spend so much time managing upward that I don't have time to fix the problem."

  o Examples of high performing organizations:

    - Bad news travels up quickly
    - Leaders are informed
    - People assume/know leaders are working on the problem
    - If help is needed from a higher level, the owners of the problem know they can ask for help.
    - Walking through a high performing organization we WITNESSED something bad happen. We turned around and walked directly to the CEO's office:

- He already knew
- He would not act on his own
- He knew his team was working on it
- He would help if asked

This is a hard culture to establish because we all want to help, but once established it allows the owner of the problem to fix it, and respects their desire, skill, and efforts.

The "secret sauce" of this culture is transparency of the problem, an understanding that the world and people are not perfect, and a willingness to help (not meddle) if asked.

> *"Leadership is solving problems. The day soldiers stop bringing you their problems is the day you have stopped leading them."*
> **General Colin Powell**

- **Ask What (the process) Before You Ask Who (the person) When Problems Arise**

    In high performing companies the leaders move away from an accusatory culture. If the workforce thinks your first reaction is to blame, they will, typically, withhold bad news.

    Go in with the assumption that the team was trying to do a good job. What stood in their way?

As with the earlier example, "who" did it is typically looking for a symptom of the problem, rather than fix the "what" which is the process that could be the root cause.

 Chapter 8 Keys:

Chapter 8: The Reality of a Strong Leader

- Leaders are responsible for understanding and conveying reality.

- Leaders must have strong listening, questioning, and communication skills.

- Leaders must be humble.

- Leaders must understand the "Commander's Intent,' the objective and reasoning behind it.

- Leaders should spend time in Quadrant 2, focusing on important but not urgent tasks like taking care of their people.

- Leaders should provide legitimate recognition and awards.

- Leaders control their attitude and attention.

9

Strengthening Your Leadership

Steps to Validate Reality

Every leader wants to believe that their leadership and organizational growth is what they project it is. Strong leaders, however, have listening posts that help them to validate "the truth."

This validation can take a wide range of forms:

- Linking metrics to the Vision, Mission, Values as translated into behaviors

- Linking metrics to each step of the Leadership System

  o Ask yourself, "What measure could be linked to each step of the Leadership System?"

- Linking leading indicator metrics to each of your objectives (which are frequently lagging indicators)

- Listening posts which you have developed can be:

  o Metrics tracked within the organization (not only by your group)

  o Individuals who can advise you (see the discussion of Mentors, below)

  o Outcomes tracked within the organization

  o Your personal ability to listen

    - What percentage of your time do you dedicate to listening?

    - How do you train yourself in and improve your ability to listen?

  o Your personal ability to ask questions, which others feel safe in answering

Defining Moments

Top leadership training groups, and top performing organizations work with leaders to understand their "defining moments." These literally can be the 10–20 seconds you get *every year* to tell people "Who you really are."

We all remember leaders who "lost it" only once or a few times, and that is what we expect or fear every time we deal with them.

A Defining Moment: Perception was never as clear to me as something I saw in graduate school. We were in a session where we went through several simple classroom leadership exercises.

We watched a movie, and then discussed the motivation of each character–very little agreement!

During one of the class sessions a man stuck his head in the door and rudely told the instructor that he had to move his class immediately, and we were in a room which was not authorized for our use. A few aggressive and harsh words were exchanged with the instructor and the man left.

The instructor continued class without telling us if we had to move. How rude was this guy?

Now nobody in the class was focused on the lesson–we were all still focused on the cave man who interrupted us, whether we really needed to move, his rudeness, and the interruption itself. For goodness' sake, we had used this same room for weeks.

A few minutes later the instructor stopped and asked us to describe the man who interrupted our class.

The class described him as:

- Angry
- Taller than he really was.
- More physically intimidating than he really was.
- Less physically attractive than he was.
- More poorly dressed than he really was.
- Less well-groomed than he really was.

It was humorous that NOBODY in class noticed that he was not even wearing shoes. The man was barefoot!

It was all a set-up, and when the instructor brought the man back, the class was very reluctant to accept him as a nice guy.

He had his "defining moment," and in our minds he blew it. In the short time we had in the remainder of the class he was unable to recover from our initial impression. In short, we did not like him, and we were not going to change our minds.

A Defining Moment: Years ago, a client, who was an incredibly compassionate man, passed away. The leadership team did not know if they could continue.

They found a path forward by each person (individually) documenting what they remembered as his "defining moments," and documenting what they wanted their personal defining moments to be remembered as in 5 years.

The tearful discussion brought the team together and cast the team's direction for the future.

In our jobs we are remembered for the actions that we take toward others. If we are kind it is remembered. If we are harsh, it is remembered, and so on.

NOBODY knows what their own defining moments are. But... the entire organization does!

Also–if you have a relationship of trust–you can ask internal mentors (see the description of the types of mentors below) to be honest with you. The answers are almost always guaranteed to surprise you. What you have intended to convey is rarely exactly what is conveyed.

Be very aware of your defining moments–they can *make or break* your organizational reputation.

Benchmarking

The Malcolm Baldrige National Quality Award defines Benchmarks as:

- Processes and results that represent best practices and performance for similar activities, inside or outside an organization's industry. Organizations engage in benchmarking to understand the current dimensions of world-class performance and to achieve discontinuous (non-incremental) or "breakthrough" improvement.

Benchmarks are one form of comparative data. Other comparative data organizations might use include industry data collected by a third party (frequently industry averages), data on competitors' performance, and comparisons with similar organizations that are in the same geographic area or that provide similar products and services in other geographic areas.

Benchmarking is not only reserved to be used at the organizational level. It can also be used for assessing your personal performance.

It is always amazing to talk to a leader and not get a robust answer to the question: "Who is very good (or the best) at what you do?"

This question does not always invoke a full answer, but it can give you an initial insight as to whether they are humble enough to even care what the answer is. If the answer is, "I don't know," I always wonder if they are even a part of any industry group, or read industry or Functional Magazines (i.e., if they are a Human Resources leader, there are numerous magazines they can read).

There are several great examples of leaders talking about benchmarking or seeking new knowledge:

- **George Patton:** The famous US Army General who faced the German General Rommel in battle, refers to reading Rommel's book in November 1944. He beat Rommel on the battlefield.

- **Albert Einstein:** The only thing more dangerous than ignorance is arrogance. *Author's note: If a leader does not study what is possible, they have both ignorance and arrogance.*

- **Stephen Hawking:** Intelligence is the ability to adapt to change.

- **Nikola Tesla:** I don't care that they stole my idea. I care that they don't have any of their own. *Author's Note: Later in this chapter we will discuss the importance of building on what you learn from benchmarking.*

- **Cyc Jouzy:** Copycats may seem good at what they are doing, but they will never find a spot at the top.

- **Kendra Scott:** Dream big and be disruptive. If you are doing the same thing as everyone else, you've already failed.

The reason the final three quotes are included is: Benchmarking should be the beginning of your thinking and development--If what you learn in benchmarking is what you have as an end-goal, you have already failed.

Conversely, only a fool would try to develop/learn/grow into something they could quickly learn from observing the world around them.

Benchmarking can be a great 'eye opener' for organizations AND leaders.

- **True?** It is rumored that when Southwest Airlines was starting, they were evaluating how they could be more effective than their competitors

  o They can't fly any faster.
  o They can't fly more hours of the day (nobody wants to board a flight at 4 am); and
  o They can't fly different routes.

  HOW can they beat the existing competition?????

- o The rumor was–the only place they could make a significant impact was on the ground "turning" an airplane at the gate. The criteria were: 1) Safety, and 2) Speed. Therefore, who should they benchmark? They benchmarked Indianapolis 500 pit crews who had the same performance criteria–Safety and Speed.
- o Meanwhile, I was at another airline. At a director's meeting someone was talking about watching Southwest turn a plane at the gate. "BOY DO THOSE GUYS HUSTLE." They also discussed that one of our airline's company policies (which we strictly enforced) was "No Running on Company Property." Our policy prevented turning a plane quickly at the gate.

- **True!!:** We've all seen middle managers who take note of the educational or experience backgrounds of the top leaders and gain that education or experience for themselves.

- **True!!:** A manufacturer of guidance for military missiles benchmarked Mary Kay Cosmetics. Why? Certainly, Mary Kay doesn't have anything to do with missiles used in war. They benchmarked them because Mary Kay had a very systematic "kitting" process to ensure all the necessary parts of every order sent out were accurate. When you put the electronic parts for a missile together to be sent to be assembled, you want to make sure all the parts are there before it is sent to the assembly line.

- **True!!:** An aircraft manufacturer felt they were THE BEST in the industry in manufacturing shop safety.

  o They worked intensively for 1 year on safety improvement, and at the end of the year felt they were pretty average!
  o Why? In that year they went out and benchmarked what other aircraft manufacturers were doing.

Knowing what others are doing MUST be only a starting point. From the quotes above you can see that you can never lead if all you do is follow.

An Example:

In 2001 Clarke American won the Baldrige Award. In attending the Baldrige Conference, they had full control of what they shared. Some winners revealed little of what they considered their "magic sauce" for being world-class. Even though Clarke American knew several of their direct competitors would be in the audience, the CEO of Clarke American announced that they would share everything. His reasoning was: "If they try to copy us, they will always be behind us."

What you learn by benchmarking should also help you know what the rate of change needs to be for you to be where you want to be, and when.

Benchmarking Summary

Knowing what the rest of the world is doing (relevant to your world), can help you understand the gap, what is possible, or what rate of change is possible. That knowledge should be used to develop a plan that will help put you and your organization ahead of your comparisons in a reasonable timeframe.

Be Careful, however. Do not assume that your comparison (a person or company) is stagnant, or that their improvement rate is constant. If I compare myself to my boss who has a master's degree, he may be continuing his/her education at a faster rate than I am, as I try to get my master's degree.

Going back to the Baldrige Definition: this is to help you achieve discontinuous (non-incremental) or "breakthrough" improvement.

Personal development is similar to organizational development. If you compare two individuals or organizations and one has lots of problems and one has no/very few problems:

Which one is high performing, and which one is low performing?

- The one with lots of problems will ALWAYS be higher performing!

    o It's not human nature to clearly identify a problem and then not do something about it

- The one with fewer problems has the same number of problems, but:

  o They don't recognize their problems
  o They do not have a systematic plan to improve/fix them
  o They aren't going to be any better tomorrow than they are today

Mentors in your leadership development

Years ago, we were working with a company of about 8,000 employees and took a half day per month to develop the top 400 leaders. This training was over 6 months, and the final session was half our message and half for the CEO to wrap-up the leadership development.

Although we understood the CEO's approach and beliefs extremely well, we did not do a good job of coordinating our final day's material with what his message would be.

We spent a lot of our last 2 hours on mentorship (being a mentor and having a mentor). As the CEO walked to the front of the room my partner and I realized we should have coordinated our message better than we did.

The CEO's first words were "Who here has a mentor?" I turned to my partner and said, "It pays to be lucky." It wasn't entirely luck, since great leaders all have someone they learn from, and someone they know is only trying to help them.

A call to personal authenticity:

As you read about these leaders and types of mentors keep their guidance in mind, however:

- Every leader is not of equal value.

- Every quote doesn't fit every situation.

- Every quote doesn't fit you or your beliefs.

- Pick one or two who fit what you want to be.

Remember, nothing true, noble, and lasting ever came from being fake, phony, or false.

Types of Mentors

There are four types of mentors, each of which has a unique purpose and contribution to your development.

Virtual Mentor

These are the leaders of the past who have documented their wisdom. Hundreds of books have been written on our founding fathers, presidents, military leaders, spiritual leaders, etc.

We have included several quotes on leadership in this book from leaders we respect.

You can't follow them all, but here are some concepts that are universal to all leaders:

Mentor Higher in Your Organization

Look for someone higher in your organization who has your best interest and growth at heart. This may not be easy, but DON'T RUSH FINDING THIS PERSON.

What could they be looking for?

- They may view you as an ambassador that they are sending forth to the future and to a time they won't see.

- They, typically, will take pride in seeing you succeed.

What are you looking for?

- A broader view of the organizational dynamics than you can gain from your position

- Wisdom

- Pitfalls or biases you need to be aware of

- Lessons from their experience that you don't have

Once you feel comfortable having that conversation with them you should try to engage them at least 15 minutes per quarter. You don't want to "overstay your welcome," but you need to take their guidance on how much of their time they will give you.

Outside Mentor

This role can be played by a wide range of people. As with the Virtual Mentor, it doesn't need to be restricted to only one person.

What could they be looking for?

- Try to find someone who wants to help you–their reward is seeing you succeed.

- They may view you as an ambassador that they are sending forth to the future and to a time they won't see.

What are you looking for?

- Find someone you trust. You need to be able to trust them not to discuss confidential issues from your workplace.

- They will have business experience which is often broader than just within your company.

- They can openly and unemotionally discuss the issues you are facing and the possible courses of action.

Note: When playing this mentor role, remember Eisenhower's quote: "Plans are worthless; Planning is essential." Many times, I planned, planned, planned with the mentee and they do the opposite of what we planned. When this happens, I am very proud of them! The planning prepared them to make a good decision, but the scenario we planned for was different from the situation they were in and they needed to make a "battlefield decision." That could not have been done without planning.

Mentor Within Your Organization

This, frequently, is one of the most valuable mentors. This can be someone in your organization you 100% trust. Previously, in a senior position, Roy was somewhere down in my organization and mentored me.

HE NEVER BROKE MY TRUST, and he knew the minute anyone knew about this relationship–it was over!

This person sees you every day and can advise you of things you are unaware of.

What could they be looking for?

- They have the boss's (your) respect.

- They can share their experience and have it utilized.

- They have access to the boss (you).

What are you looking for?

- Feedback can be immediate (but NEVER in public.)

- They can tell you things no other category of mentor can tell you:

  o Feedback on your daily behavior
  o Reaction to your decisions
  o Impact of your decisions

Mentor Summary

Obviously, you have the final decision of who you listen to and what you act on.

A favorite memory is when I expressed a very strong position on a key issue to my leaders. The Mentor from Within My Organization followed me into my office and shut the door. I told him, "Don't say anything. I mean that, and I meant to do that."

I appreciated his concern, and he appreciated that in the final analysis I had to live with the decision and impact. That issue was one I was not willing to equivocate on.

To summarize what each of these mentors give you:

- **Virtual Mentor:**

    o Wisdom from the ages. These quotes are easy to find, but the application to your own leadership actions is much harder.

    o **Timing:** As you wish.

- **Mentor Higher in Your Organization:**

    o Wisdom and lessons learned from the culture you live in.

    o **Timing:** 15 minutes per quarter

- **Outside Mentor:**

    o Wisdom comes from a broader base of experience than you have access to.

    o Note: This can be very valuable, but do not forget that they do not understand the culture of the environment you live in.

- o **Timing:** 15-30 minutes 6+ times per year

- **Mentor Within Your Organization:**
  - o Real-time feedback of the impact of your leadership actions.
  - o **Timing:** As needed–this can be several times a day, but at least monthly

Use of any of these mentors requires you to have the humility to listen, and to do something different based on their feedback.

Always remember, the final decision on your positions, communication, and actions are yours.

Continuously Improving Your Leadership–Measuring Your Own Performance and Improvement Plans

Throughout this book we have discussed a leader's requirement to improve.

That improvement should not be catch-as-catch-can, but you should use a documented approach, such as tracking your performance using the matrix below.

This is your personal evaluation and is not typically shared with anyone else. It reflects the humility to continuously work on the effectiveness of your leadership, and to look for areas and ways to improve.

Designing Your Matrix to Monitor Your Leadership Growth:

It is certainly up to you whether you ever share this with anyone. At a minimum, track your own progress, and always keep in mind humility and a passionate desire for results– including your own leadership growth.

- The left column can be the factors around your Leadership System

  o See the examples in the Appendix and the steps to develop your own Leadership System

- Don't forget the connecting arrows, which cannot be delegated

  o Getting this right can not only make or break you as a leader, but can impact your organizational image and reputation

- Another column can be added to the right column for each level of the organization

  o This can allow the leaders at any level to translate how they will measure their own performance

- Goals and/or activities may be slightly different for each level

  o The measures may also be different, and should be linked to that level's goals and span of control

Leadership System Attributes	Leaders at every level must:
Understand stakeholders' expectations	Adhere to stakeholder engagement plan.
Set Direction and Plan	Set strategic directions for Business Unit Guide the organization to evolve the scorecard and strategic initiatives.
Communicate and Build Commitment	Schedule for communication. Communicate strategy through focused sessions in all areas.
Organize, Align, and Allocate Resources	Prioritize allocation of resources for key initiatives.
Build, Motivate, Empower Team for Accelerated Change	Evolve empowerment plan and implement.
Review and Adjust to Achieve Plan	Review progress on the scorecard and measures and strategic initiatives every month. Identify gap areas and seek solutions from each member.
Create a Culture of High Performance	Assign critical positions to high potential performers.
Develop, Reward, and Recognize Employees	Track status of high potential/performing employees.
Adapt to New Challenges and Raise the Bar	Continuously scan business environment and set stretch targets.
Innovate, Share and Learn	Encourage idea patenting in the organization.

Be a Role Model	Walk the Talk and Demonstrate exemplary ethical conduct.

 ## Chapter 9 Keys:

Chapter 9: Strengthening Your Leadership

- Leaders can improve their effectiveness by using techniques like walking around and listening, posting results, acknowledging, accepting, and appreciating (AAA) their team, and using data visualization.

- Leaders must define their "Trust Profile" and communicate it to their team.

- Leaders should celebrate mistakes as opportunities for learning and growth.

- Leaders should identify their "defining moments" and strive to make them positive.

- Benchmarking is a valuable tool for learning from others, but leaders should strive to go beyond what they learn from benchmarking.

- Leaders should seek out mentors from various sources.

- Leaders should track their own performance and develop improvement plans.

10

Military–Sports–Business

There are obvious ties between leadership and the three items in the chapter title and much has been written about the obvious similarities. What about the differences? Generally speaking, sports is not "To the death!" and neither is business. What about the substantial differences in execution? For example, on game day in high school and in college, it was normal to have the band, cheerleaders, and bleachers full of fans from both teams cheering on each side. Do you have that in your business?

In the military, it was normal for us to communicate with symbols, with musical instruments, with flags, lights, and many other tools. Is it normal in your business to communicate in these ways?

In chapter 8, we promised to talk more about "momentum shifts" and how to orchestrate one for your business team. You may remember the scene in the Mel Gibson movie, "The Patriot," when the lead character takes the repaired flag and turns the tide in the climactic battle scene by running forward (charging) when his group was being routed and was in a disorganized retreat. His heroic action sparked an emotional response and a renewed energy for his troops. They won the day.

On the real field of battle during the US Civil War, a teacher from Bowdoin College, Lt. Col Joshua Lawrence Chamberlain, pulled off a momentum shift that saved the Union Army at Gettysburg and put them on the path to victory in the war. Out of ammunition and with a group of highly disgruntled soldiers, Chamberlain's decision to charge down the hill known as Little Round Top was a defining moment for many participants. Chamberlain was awarded the Medal of Honor for his actions under fire that day and I highly recommend that you, as a leader, watch the clip[4] below as an instruction for leading when all the factors are going in the wrong direction:

Desperation is the mother of invention!

You don't have to be desperate to orchestrate a momentum shift. If you, as a leader, are tuned to reality and see that the factors are going against you and your team, you can insert an emotional energy lift and turn things around. Trust your people. When you and your team are connected deeply to each other and to the mission, the emotional energy is easy to access. HINT: Without this deep sense of connectedness, your team may not be able to muster the energy to keep fighting, much less the commitment to renewed vigor. The best leaders model the way.

---

[4] https://youtu.be/KBowND4qACI?si=BqXiHsKmLvuqIzII

In the USA, we've borrowed much from our military traditions and extended those borrowed traditions to our sports teams. American Football is essentially a mock battlefield with opposing armies battling to take ground from each other and to defend ground against the others' attack. It's not surprising that we see the best teams leveraging "military traditions" and using many of the same words such as strategy, tactics, offense, defense, special teams, etc. We also rely heavily on team leaders on the field. The team "captains" are the designated on-field leaders. Coaches with perennial high-performing teams are highlighted in the appendix to this book with breakdowns of coaching philosophies and values. Even if you are not into sports, if you are leading a team, you'll want to familiarize yourself with these concepts.

In team sports, usually the coach is not on the field during the contest.

As a coach, your primary job is to get your team ready to play and win against the competitors on your schedule. Just like in business, it is critically important to get the best players available into the right positions on the team and to help them grow and develop while planning to compete against the next team. Unifying your team and keeping them united in the face of negative factors throughout the season is challenging. Building a winning program over many seasons is impressive. As business leaders, we study the coaches that have figured out how to get the best from their players over the long haul and do our best to apply wisdom from those arenas to our own.

Even at the professional level of most sports, ongoing development and training are important investments for the teams and for the individuals. As in the military, where the training is nearly continuous from day one, professional sports teams are always advancing with the idea that each player can improve and as the individuals improve, the team inevitably improves.

One of the most important aspects of "player potential" is the "coachability" of the player. If the player is not coachable, we typically don't want them on our teams. If your team member is not coachable in your business team, you'll typically see someone who is never willing to be accountable for inaction, or bad actions they've taken and will inevitably say it's someone else's fault. Sometimes you see this with amazing athletes, but you won't want them on your team. More importantly, the other members of the team won't want them on the team.

There are obvious strengths and capacities in each individual. There are many not-so-obvious inherent attributes. Coachability is just one example that's not obvious but can be discerned quickly. Work ethic, grit or resiliency, integrity, loyalty, team-first attitude versus me-first—each of these falls into the non-obvious, unseen attribute columns, but they are very important.

Are you building a high-performing team? If you are, then you'll need to build a strong foundation on a leadership system that can capture your wisdom and that of your current team and distribute that body of wisdom forward to those who come after you.

John was recently on a trip to Cincinnati and saw these values reflected on the walls of a professional baseball team – The Cincinnati Reds.

It's clear they need talented players, but their selection criteria go way beyond what "Can Be Seen". In the section called "Cannot Be Seen" – listed are major sections on Personality – improvement, consistency, maturity, adjustment, stability, temperament, disposition; Attitude – desire, drive, willingness, hunger, ambition; Mental - intelligence, baseball sense, teachability, knowledge of the game; Winner – stomach, heart, competitor, pride; Background – family, habits.

As leaders we can certainly learn from this example.

Chapter 10 Keys:

Chapter 10: Military–Sports–Business

- There are similarities and differences between leadership in the military, sports, and business.

- Leaders can learn from the military about the importance of momentum shifts and the use of after-action reviews.

- Leaders can learn from sports about the importance of teamwork, coaching, and building a winning culture.

- Leaders should select team members based not only on talent but also on character and values.

11

Conclusion

We started with the question, "What is a leader?"

Anyone in your organization can be called on to lead at almost any time. A leader must have agency – the leader makes decisions and chooses a path for the followers. This agency comes with risks and great responsibilities. Will that person be prepared? In most organizations, the answer to that is no. But some organizations, such as the military, great sports programs, and some exceptional companies do spend the time and money to create a set of expectations and an approach to leading that inspires high performance. And, for many of those organizations, the high level of performance is sustained beyond the tenure of the top leader, whether that leader is a top-ranked officer in the military, a great coach, or a famous CEO. Getting to high performance is rare. Sustaining it is even more exceptional.

We recognized that leadership means many things to many people.

What does it mean to you? What does it mean in your organization? We believe that needs to be defined by you and by your group of leaders at every level in the organization – you decide what it means and what behaviors are expected and what behaviors should never be tolerated for you and for your company. You and your team can start with these leadership systems shared in this book and use them as a guide or model, but the work to wrestle with the mission, vision, and values alone are enough to get people engaged and back on a path to good, steady performance. It is here, in this work and these discussions that your unique culture is revealed and optimized for the future. It may not be what you want it to be at the start. We guarantee that it will NEVER be what you want it to be without engaging in the work to set the foundation. Systems move from order to disorder. This is the law of entropy. Stewardship is required – continuously.

We saw that vision and visibility are keys to driving performance.

Looking back to understand what happened in the past and having a context to understand what is happening now, gives a leader a place to stand and see what will happen in the future. Vision is important. Communicating the vision is challenging and yet, clarity is a game changer. As a leader, you are being looked at all the time and your behaviors are in alignment with those championed or they are not. Weakness here is very bad for anyone in a leadership role. "Rules for thee, but not for me" does not play well in the current era.

How do you use this book?

This book has been compiled from over 90 years of leadership experience, and access to some great leaders.

As such, this is not information you can absorb or fully apply with one reading or a short time. To use this book to the fullest, consider some of the following steps:

- Reflect on each lesson or Winner's Circle and determine whether or how it fits you.

- Make notes as to your leadership strengths

- Make notes as to what you would like to improve

- Make notes as to how to improve

  o This should include the steps and their importance
  o Major steps, like developing your own leadership system will require others to be involved and take months to implement

- Make notes on an overall timeframe for each improvement

  o **Warning:** Do not try to do too much too fast–that will guarantee failure

- Think about how you would measure progress in each step. This could include:

- o Step
- o Measure
- o Personal Reflection

    - Note: We have seen leaders who are using a leadership system take 15 minutes each Friday to reflect on their progress

      If you do something like this, it is important to be honest about your OFI's (Opportunities for Improvement) without being too tough on yourself. This takes time and does not happen quickly. More progress may take more time or trial and error so take the time and then adjust.

- o Next Steps

    - Timing
    - Expected outcome
    - Measures
    - The role for the others involved

As with all "gifts" the recipient has full control of what to do with it.

- Some will put the book down and not think about it again

- Some will use it and develop a lifetime plan

- Some will develop a simple plan

- Some will use it to informally reflect on key issues

Whatever you decide to do, you are the key beneficiary of your actions. Follow through and repeat these exercises regularly and you'll most likely find that many others, long after you've left the organization are also beneficiaries. It is an opportunity to create a legacy of leadership.

"Fruit on the Tree"

Over the years, both of your authors have seen companies apply the ideas in this book very well and those companies have achieved high performance. We've seen these tools used to effect turnarounds in the military, in the Fortune 500, and in global enterprises. These ideas and tools work for everyone that drives through them to get to a unified team of leaders with clarity on the vision, mission, values, and behaviors that win for them. There is no need to have managers that don't know what is expected of them. There's no need to have people on the payroll that don't know how their jobs affect the bottom line of the company. No need to have people who are "busy" but never seem to get things done. A leadership system is the key to getting the culture set for high performance and the key to getting your people engaged and excited about what you are building together.

In the Afterword right after this chapter, Dave Fox shares how he and his leaders used this method to save his hospital in a very tough market. At the beginning of the book, you read the story of how David Spong used these ideas to win two Baldrige awards at two very different organizations. This works.

Reflections

On reflection, this is a book I (Walt) never would have imagined in 1985, the year I started my military career. The leadership system I entered was well-established, remarkably mature, and deadly effective. In late 1992, I began the "civilian" phase of my work-life and found nothing like the leadership system I had unknowingly grown up in as the child of a career military man and as a high school and collegiate football player. No real personal development training or classes and little to no leadership training were available within some of the biggest companies in the USA at the time (and I worked at Fidelity, Gannett, and TRW!).

With the contents of this book and the associated workbook, it is my hope that you will embrace the idea of a systematic approach to sharing wisdom and knowledge throughout your organization and to an active countering of cultural rot or cultural entropy. I know from personal experience that one can grab this material and insert it anywhere in a large organization and start to influence the surrounding work groups very positively, while you build a safe, fun environment for your group within the larger group. It won't happen overnight, but the impact when it happens is profound and far reaching. Think of the ripples in the pond that are created when you throw one stone in–how far out do the ripples extend beyond the point of entry? You can be that kind of influencer in your company's legacy.

Please let us know if you found value in this–your authors would love to hear and share or amplify your win stories, and we would love to know that your leadership system–unique to you and your group–left a good probability of sustained success and high-performance long after you depart from your current leadership role.

Chapter 11: Conclusion

- Leaders must define what leadership means in their organization and establish clear expectations for behavior.

- Leaders should use the book as a guide for reflection, self-assessment, and development.

- Leaders have an opportunity to create a legacy of leadership.

- A leadership system is key to creating a culture of high performance and engagement.

AFTERWORD

Transforming Culture

Transforming Organizational Culture As A Gateway To Performance Excellence

Dave Fox, President (retired)
Advocate Good Samaritan Hospital
Malcolm Baldrige National Quality Award,
2010 Recipient

Assessing the Culture

In 2004, Advocate Good Samaritan Hospital (GSAM) performed a strategic assessment that confirmed that the hospital's future was at risk in the highly competitive DuPage County (Illinois) marketplace. An honest review identified significant challenges confronting the organization:

- Patient satisfaction was generally mediocre and in our outpatient departments that served a majority of our patients, patient satisfaction was at the 7th percentile.

- Associate engagement was mediocre in many departments with the result that it was difficult to attract and retain top caliber staff.

- Physician engagement among the 900-member medical staff was low and relationships with some elected physician leaders ranged from ambivalent to antagonistic.

- Clinical outcomes were very good in cardiology, neonatology, and emergency/trauma medicine while being mostly average in other departments.

- Due to a lack of capital, facilities were outdated and slipping further behind in the local "medical arms race"; and,

- Patient volumes were stagnant resulting in inadequate net operating income.

The Impact of the Culture

In light of these challenges to the organization it was unlikely that incremental improvements in our outcomes would be enough to create a more positive trajectory for the future. What was needed was an overhaul of GSAM's vision, business model and culture.

In deciding to create a new future, we recognized that simply changing and improving how we currently operated the business would not be nearly enough. We needed to transform every aspect of the hospital.

- In our view, *"change"* was about doing better what we already knew how to do.

- *"Transformation"* was about doing what wasn't currently possible unless or until we changed how our leadership related to, and engaged with, our physicians, associates and patients. Transforming the hospital would require us to tap into and unleash the passions of our physicians and associates.

The Journey to Change the Culture

We knew that due to a lack of capital we could not compete in the local *medical arms race*. So instead, we embarked on a journey to dramatically differentiate GSAM's services and outcomes for patients, associates, physicians, and the community.

An opportunity for us was the reality that many of our specialty physicians practiced at one or two other hospitals. We believed that if we were successful at differentiating our services specialty physicians would shift more of their patients to our hospital.

We launched our transformational journey by creating a new vision, a new and more powerful "culture" and a new management model that enabled high levels of transparency, alignment, and accountability.

Having been inspired by Jim Collins' 2003 book, *Good To Great*, we decided to call our transformation, "Moving from Good to Great" (G2G). The first step in this journey was to create a new vision and strategic intention for the hospital. Our new vision was, "to provide an exceptional patient experience marked by superior clinical outcomes and service." This vision would be energized by a strategic intention for the hospital "to become the best place for physicians to practice, associates to work and patients to receive care."

We believed that every organization has a unique culture, and yet for most organizations the existing culture wasn't intentionally created so much as it was a result of the people, practices and policies of its leadership. While it is common for senior leaders to announce new visions and strategies many of these change initiatives fail because leaders do not grasp that the new strategic plan requires a new culture to catalyze its efforts and enhance the possibility of success.

We understood at the outset that our journey to organizational excellence would require a transformation of our culture. The current culture of our organization contributed to our inadequate performance and outcomes.

Strengthening Behaviors

"Culture" is sometimes described as the observable values and behaviors that exist within the organization. We understood that our current culture was producing mediocre levels of engagement with our staff and mostly average outcomes for outpatients. So, the first step in transforming our culture was to create an explicit set of 25 required behaviors for all associates, including leaders.

After sharing those Standards of Behaviors individually with each of our 2,000 associates, we required them to embrace this new way of "being" within the hospital.

Strengthening Evaluations and the Team

As part of the rollout of the new behavioral standards, we ranked our associates as High, Middle, or Low performers. For the 10% of associates who were rated as low performers, we advised them that they either needed to improve their behaviors or prepare to leave the organization. During the first year of our G2G journey, over half of our low-rated employees departed the organization.

Our decision to focus on low performers in part reflected our knowledge of the annual Gallup Engagement Survey which classified employees as "engaged," "not engaged," or "actively disengaged." In a recent national survey, Gallup found that 22% of

employees were engaged, 51% were not engaged and 17% were actively disengaged.

We also modified how we recruited associates. We were determined to hire new associates who already embodied our standards of behavior. Previously, we hired for skill and hoped for culture fit. Our new hiring processes were designed to screen for skill and then hire for culture fit.

We also created departmental peer interviewing teams comprised of high performers who participated in the interviewing of potential new associates.

Strengthening Objectives and Leadership

The last initial step in our creation of a new culture involved our middle managers and senior executives. We recognized that our current mediocre outcomes were the product of managers and senior leaders not being individually accountable for improvement in specific outcomes. The existing merit pay program for managers mostly evaluated managers for achieving departmental budgets.

There were a few other objectives that explicitly impacted a manager's performance rating and pay raise. In place of this somewhat loose performance review policy, we created objective, measurable goals for each of the six newly created key result areas of: 1) clinical outcomes; 2) associate engagement; 3) physician engagement; 4) patient satisfaction; 5) growth; and 6) funding our future.

For each department, objective measurable goals were then established along with predetermined levels of outcome that translated into grades to be used in the annual performance review and pay hike process for managers and senior leaders.

Results and Performance Transparency

Manager and senior leader performance scores were posted each month on the hospital's proprietary intranet so that all managers and senior leaders could observe how other members of the management team were performing. The hospital president's report card was also posted and distributed to all managers, board members, and physician leaders at the end of every month.

The Impact of Strengthening the Culture

During the first two years of our G2G journey (2004-2006) our outcomes improved dramatically.

The improvement in outcomes resulted from numerous changes we had made to how we operated our business.

- Critical to the success of our new business approaches was our new culture.

- By 2006, our outpatient satisfaction exceeded the 99th percentile; associate and physician engagement were approaching the 90th percentile; and our clinical outcomes were improving across the board.

- By 2009, we were recognized for the first time as a Top 100 Hospital (awarded by Truven), and by 2012 we were recognized by Health Grades as one of America's 50 best hospitals.

- In 2010, we became a recipient of a Malcolm Baldrige National Quality Award.

From 2006 to 2011, our inpatient volumes increased significantly as specialty physicians chose to direct more of their surgical procedures to GSAM.

The Journey in Hindsight–Our Core Competency Was Key

In the early years of our transformation journey, we decided that we needed not just to satisfy our physicians, associates and patients, but we needed to build *loyalty* among all of the constituencies of our hospital community.

As our engagement outcomes continued to improve, we determined that our 'core competency' was *to build loyal relationships*.

This competency also reflected our belief that relationships are the foundation for accomplishment. It was the development of trusting relationships with our physicians and associates that enabled us to make significant and continuous improvements in our clinical practices that generated upward leaps in the patient experience as well as our risk-adjusted clinical outcomes.

There is no doubt that these significant breakthroughs in outcomes across all key performance areas were enabled and catalyzed by the hospital's new culture.

"Relationship is the foundation for accomplishment."

Dave Fox
President (retired)
Advocate Good Samaritan Hospital
Malcolm Baldrige National Quality Award Recipient

Appendices

Example Of Using A Leadership System

Setting Vision and Values

Example from Prince William Water (PWW) -- Our MVV and key Areas of Excellence (AOE) provide the foundation and roadmap for the Senior Leadership Team (SLT) to guide the workforce. The SLT sets and deploys the organization's vision and values (Figure P.1-2) through the Strategic Integration System in Figure 2.0-1. The Board of Directors (BOD) sets a 10-year vision which includes the key AOE, and we ensure that this is integrated into each employee's goals.

The BOD recently updated the vision for 2016-2025. We held a strategic planning session that included 50 leaders within the organization (the SLT and other leaders) to update the supporting strategic plan.

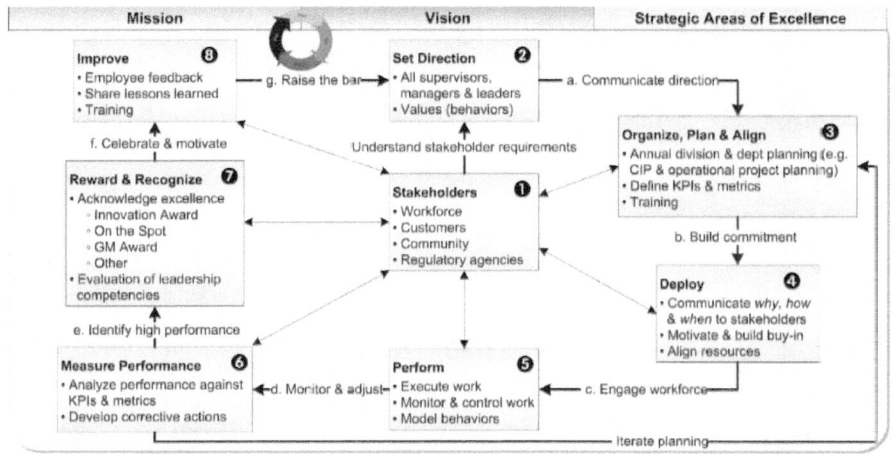

Strategic objectives are reviewed, and annual business and action plans are developed for each key AOE.

The SLT deploys our values through the LS. Our values are embedded in our goals, training, and performance management system (PMS). All leaders are required to model behavior and are held accountable through the PMS. We communicate, build commitment, and engage the workforce on a day-to-day basis to reflect those values. Deployment examples are in the Leader Communication Model. The personal actions of our SLT also reflect a commitment to those values. As an example, our Customer Service Management Team will adjust their schedules to accommodate customers outside of normal business hours.

Our vision and values are deployed to suppliers and partners through the terms and conditions of our contracts. In setting direction, we consider all stakeholders and customers and promote our mission through various communications like our award-winning website. Promoting Legal and Ethical Behavior Members of the SLT demonstrate their commitment to legal and ethical behavior by holding employees accountable through the Performance Management System.

We promote an organizational ethical environment through evaluating their actions. We use a 16-step approach for legal and ethical compliance. This system has both proactive and responsive cycles. For example, any employee can raise an ethics-related concern by using the Fraud Prevention and Reporting Hotline. Systematic approaches promote a legal and ethical environment and are reviewed annually through the Strategic Planning Process. We comply with state and federal regulations that include, but are not limited to, the Safe Drinking Water Act, the Clean Water Act, and the Clean Air Act.

Example Of How To Develop Your Own Leadership System

There are several steps to developing and using your own Leadership System. It is key that this process is endorsed by the senior leaders (Step 1), is tested and improved (Steps 2 through 7), and is linked to the competencies desired in the organization (Steps 8 through 12).

1. Senior leaders must buy-in and develop the Leadership System model

2. Conduct leadership system exercise to draft the Leadership System model

3. Think on it and refine

4. Test with next level down (focus groups)

5. Act on suggestions from test

6. Develop a communication plan

7. Roll out leadership system

8. Develop leadership competencies

9. Map competencies to training to identify strengths and gaps

10. Link leadership competencies to hiring process and performance management

11. Link to succession plans at senior levels and development plans for all leaders

12. Incorporate into strategic planning to ensure capabilities and capacity, financial resources

Explaining Each Step Further:

1. Senior leaders must buy-in and develop the Leadership System model

Agree on the definition of a leader and a Leadership System

Sample Definition of a Leader and Leadership System

The term "leader," as it is used in reference to the Leadership System, refers to all leaders at any level in the organization. This is not only limited to the top leaders (the head of the organization and that person's direct reports– which are referred to as "Senior Leadership"), but includes every leader supervising at least one other person. In some organizations key positions are considered leaders even if they do not supervise, and in other organizations all employees are considered leaders.

The term "leadership system" refers to how leadership is exercised, formally and informally, throughout the organization; it is the basis for, and the way key decisions are made, communicated, and carried out. It includes structures and mechanisms for decision making; two-way communication; selection and development of leaders and managers; and reinforcement of values, ethical behavior, directions, and performance expectations.

An effective leadership system respects the capabilities and requirements of workforce members and other stakeholders, and it sets high expectations for performance and performance improvement. It builds loyalties and teamwork based on the organization's vision and values and the pursuit of shared goals. It encourages and supports initiative and appropriate risk taking, subordinates organizational structure to purpose and function, and avoids chains of command that require long decision paths. An effective leadership system includes mechanisms for the leaders to conduct self-examination, receive feedback, and improve.

Agree that leadership must be exercised at all levels in the organization.

Agree that, once developed, a Leadership System will:

- Clearly set expectations for the roles and responsibilities of leaders as they lead

- Help the organization:

  o Screen/interview/hire potential leaders
  o Evaluate current leaders
  o Promote current leaders
  o Develop current and future leaders

    - Define how leaders spend their time and what they cannot delegate
    - Be an approach to continuously evolving and improving
    - Codify and deploy the wisdom and the approach of the current and past leaders
    - Create the culture and behavior for the organization
    - Be a Role model for other process development activities in the organization

2. Conduct leadership system exercise to draft the Leadership System model

Prior to this session:

- If they are not documented, develop and document (at a minimum in draft form):

  o Vision
  o Mission

o   Values

o   Behaviors

Review the stakeholder groups and the requirements of each group.

Discuss and agree on the key points of #1 above.

Discuss the Characteristics of Great Leaders and other leadership views.

For Example, brainstorm:

-   What are the characteristics of great leaders?
-   What are the characteristics of great leaders which cannot be (easily) taught?
-   What are the responsibilities of leaders which cannot be delegated (i.e., every leader at every level must do these things)?
-   What are the cultural characteristics or beliefs that SLs have emphasized to all employees?
-   What are the cultural characteristics or beliefs that SLs have emphasized to all leaders (if they are different than your answers to question 4)?
-   What are the processes in place to ensure that appropriate communication goes down to every employee?
-   What are the processes in place to ensure that bad news flows up quickly?

- What will future leaders need to be stronger in than in the past?

Review Several Examples of Leadership Systems

These are available from Baldrige National Quality Award Recipients (Most of whom have a Leadership System). These can be found at:

Baldrige Award Recipients Listing | NIST

Break out into 3 groups, each of which designs a Leadership System

- Approximately 1 Hour

  o NO SHARING BETWEEN GROUPS!

    Each group briefs their Leadership System to the whole team

    The entire team works to design one leadership System for the organization, taking the best parts from each breakout team.

3. **Think about the Leadership Systems and refine if needed**

Leaders take 2–3 weeks to think about it, review it 1:1 with decision influencers, and discuss changes.

This typically means taking the draft Leadership System and presenting it to several groups of employees at all levels. Document their understanding, concerns, and comments.

This typically does not change the Leadership System (although it may), but the comments usually help in how the system is described to the organization as it is rolled out.

The leadership team agrees on any changes. This step typically changes the Leadership System slightly, if at all.

4. **Test with next level down (focus groups)**

Hold a session with 10–20 employees and present the current version of the Leadership System

This should be a cross-section of the workforce and listen to their comments.

5. **Act on suggestions from test**

Typically, the test does not mean changes to the system, but frequently it highlights the clarity of terms, and impacts the overall roll-out approach.

6. **Develop a communication plan**

Design a communication plan which reflects the leader's reasoning in #1 above, and fits with the organizational culture.

Test the communication plan and changes appropriately.

7. Roll-out leadership system

It has been our experience that briefing the Leadership System in a waterfall fashion, where every leader briefs their direct reports has NO VALUE. It is viewed as a "spectator sport."

What we have found does impact each leader is using a workbook which requires each leader to *write down* how they will achieve each step.

Then if the workbook is reviewed by each person's direct supervisor within a short time it can be the genesis of critical conversations, including:

- What was written
- The supervisor's input regarding content, accuracy and completeness
- What development could strengthen the leader's overall performance

8. Develop leadership competencies

Once the Roll-out is started, Human Resources (HR) should develop (if they do not already exist) leadership competencies which can be used to measure a leader's performance.

9. **Map competencies to training to identify strengths and gaps**

HR should develop a way to assess each competency in a leader and develop a method to strengthen performance where there are gaps.

10. **Link leadership competencies to hiring process and performance management**

HR Changes the hiring process and the performance evaluation process to reflect how you want leaders to perform.

Linking Leadership System To Performance

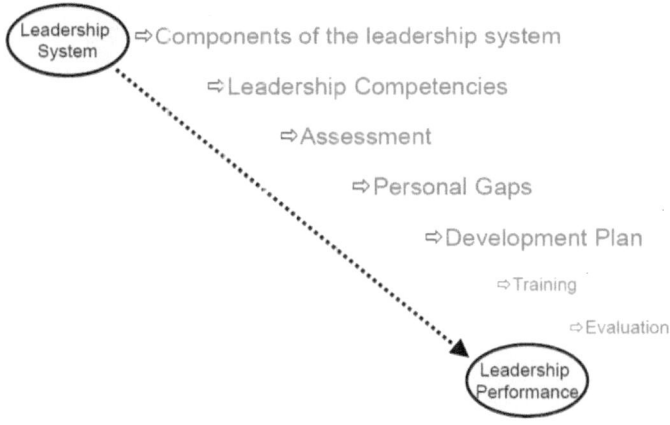

This should be rolled out over more than one evaluation cycle so nobody is "surprised" by these changes

- Cycle 1–test the evaluation process and let people know what their evaluation would be once the system is fully implemented next cycle.

- Cycle 2–make improvements from Cycle 1 and make it a part of a leader's evaluation

11. **Link to succession plans at senior levels and development plans for all leaders**

12. **Incorporate the Leadership System into strategic planning (and other areas) to ensure capabilities and capacity, financial resources**

- Review the Leadership System annually to determine if there should be (typically very small) changes

- Ensure the Leadership System is embedded in all appropriate organizational documents, such as:

    o Recruiting Documents
    o Onboarding Documents
    o Leadership Promotions
    o Leadership Evaluations
    o Strategic Planning

Additional Examples Of Leadership Systems

Health Care: Charleston Area Medical Center

*Authors' Note: The components of this system are shown in "call outs"
which typically all Leadership Systems Contain.*

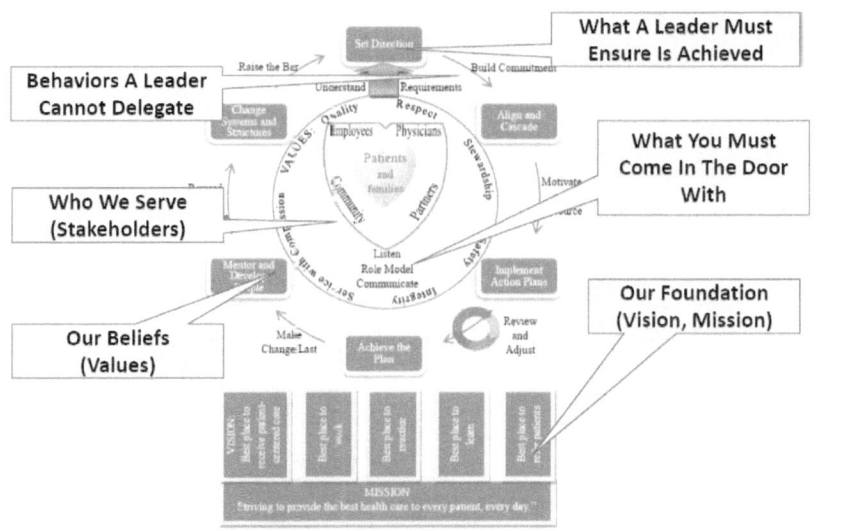

Manufacturing: Boeing Airlift and Tanker

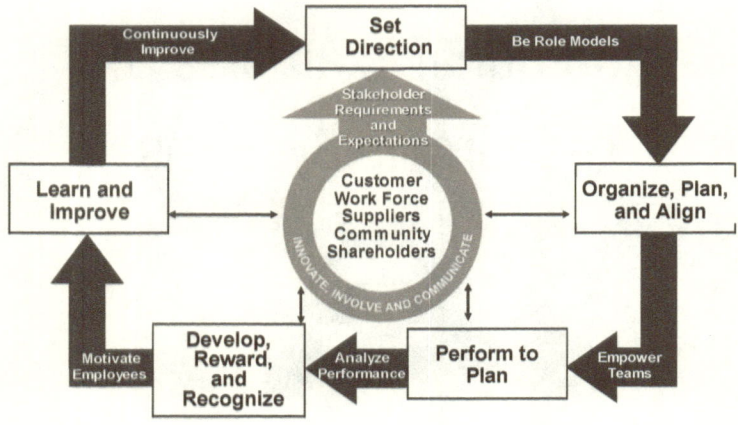

Service: Don Chalmers Ford, Albuquerque

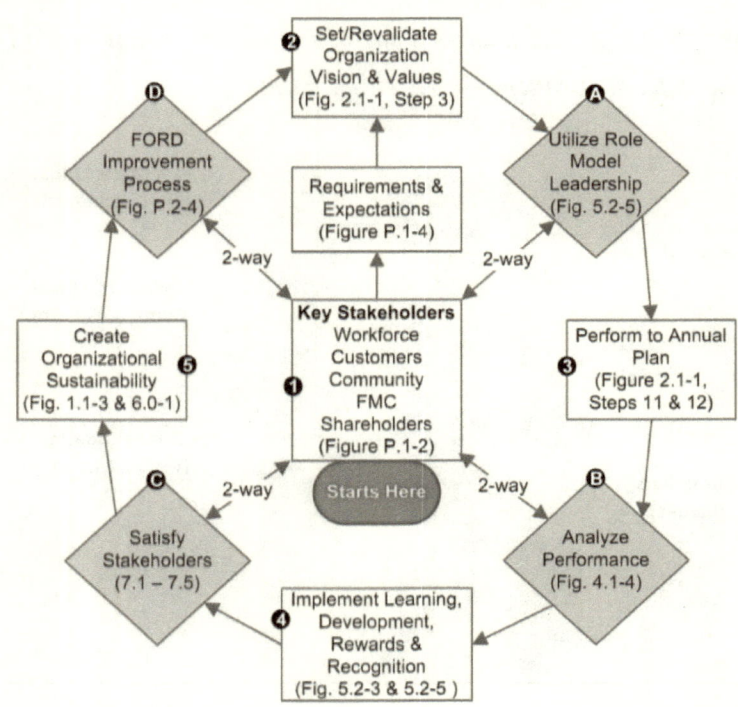

Health Care: Advocate Good Samaritan Hospital

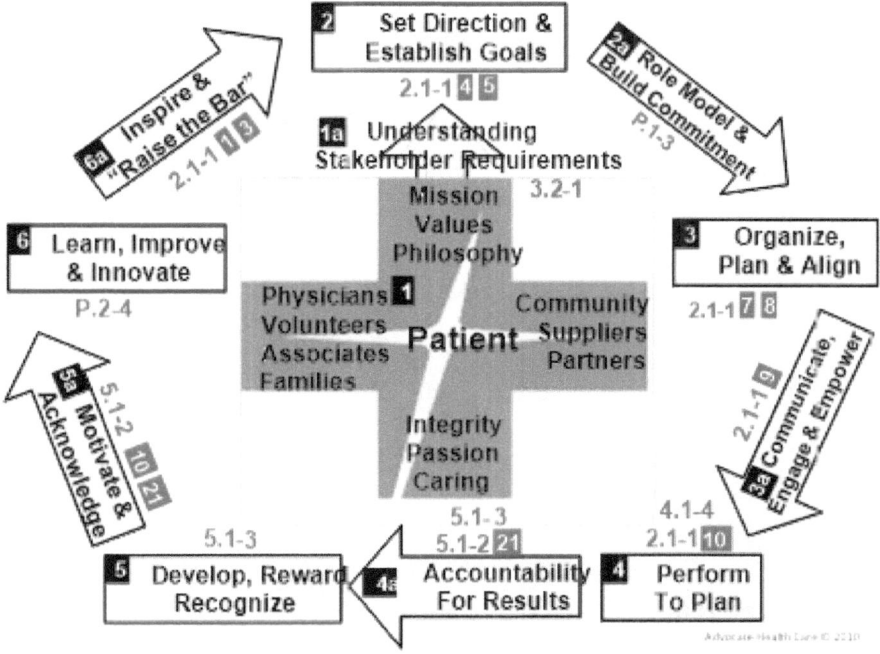

Examples Of Behavior Standards

Reprinted From Baldrige Users Guide Ninth Edition Page 21

Lafayette General Medical Center

(Recipient of Louisiana's Top-Quality Award)

Authors' Note: Walking into Lafayette General Medical Center you quickly feel the positive atmosphere. This place felt different! The behaviors they embrace (shown below) are comprehensive and are well known by everybody. They are even posted in a main hallway as you enter the main building.

In working sessions, it is difficult to tell "who represents which function," because the ownership for success is universal. For example, NOBODY EVER SAYS "that's not my job."

Note that every behavior starts with "I Will."

LGMC Employee Service Standards of Behavior

As an employee of Lafayette General Health, I believe that there is no higher responsibility than to provide and ensure a high quality and a caring environment for our patients, customers, and coworkers. I know that I am only one person, but I also know that it only takes one person to make a difference, either positive or negative. When I choose to work within this system, I am choosing to embrace the following SERVICE standards and behavioral values in order to promote the mission and vision of our system. I will be both committed to and accountable for demonstrating supportiveness, etiquette, respect, vibrancy, integrity, communication, and excellence in service delivery by adhering to the behaviors specified in this document.

Supportiveness

- I will welcome new employees to the system.

- I will be a team player and work collaboratively to help others, including those outside of my department.

- I will avoid using the phrase, "That's not my job."

- I will recognize, praise, and thank my fellow workers as well as my customers and patients.

- I will have a mentor and be a mentor.

- I will promote confidence in LGH by speaking well of my co-workers, medical staff, and any part of our system, especially, but not only, in front of patients.

Etiquette

- I will use AIDET always.

- I will use proper phone etiquette by identifying myself, and the department, followed by a pleasant greeting.

- I will follow the 10/5 rule: acknowledging the person at 10 feet away with a smile, saying "hello" at 5 feet away.

- I will allow patients, customers, and guests on and off an elevator first.

- I will help lost guests and new employees by escorting them to their destination. I will avoid merely pointing in a general direction.

Respect

- I will be mindful of what my appearance portrays by wearing clothes that are clean, neat and in good repair.

- I will respect my coworkers by ensuring that my workspace is clean, neat, and organized prior to leaving each day or night.

- I will respect my patient's dignity. I will knock before entering patient rooms and appropriately cover patients being transferred or transported.

- I will respect religious and cultural diversity, as well as those with special needs.

Vibrancy

- I will make a conscious decision to have a positive, willing, and flexible attitude each day.

- I will be attentive and alert, ready to help at all times. I will promptly acknowledge people who approach me or my desk.

- I will wear my name badge properly on the upper part of my body where it proudly communicates who I am and what I do.

- I will promote a nurturing, healing, and safe physical environment by removing clutter, ensuring cleanliness and keeping equipment in working order. I will report any damaged equipment or unsafe situations immediately.

- I will care for my own health, well-being, and emotions so that I can better care for others.

- I will embrace change by contributing and being open to new ideas and approaches. Further, I will avoid using phrases like, "But that's how we've always done it."

Integrity

- I will lead by example.

- I will ensure the privacy and validity of all medical records, correspondence, and confidential dialogue.

- I will proactively seek opportunities for continued learning, as well as professional and personal growth.

- I will be fiscally responsible by not wasting hospital time, resources, or equipment.

Communication

- I will explain things in a way people can understand.

- I will remember that body language is a powerful communicator. I will smile and demonstrate an open, friendly posture.

- I will take the time to listen—to employees, patients, customers, administrators, guests, etc.--making eye contact when possible.

- I will give and receive constructive criticism in a timely manner and turn it into an opportunity to improve.

- I will take the time to read hospital and system communications (emails, flyers, bulletins, policies, electronic boards, etc.) to stay informed of responsibilities, changes, and events. I will avoid repeatedly using the phrase, "I didn't know."

- I will ensure that employees and patients are informed and updated about changes. Further, I will foster participation in decision making to the greatest extent possible.

- I will avoid using communication devices (cell phones, text, internet, iPod) for personal reasons during work time. (Policy V-D7)

Excellence (in service delivery)

- I will convey concern and compassion as well as a willingness to serve.

- I will respond to all calls for assistance in a timely manner (1-2 min.) and provide periodic progress reports.

- I will know and utilize the ACT Complaint Resolution/Service Recovery Policy when presented with any complaint(s) from patients, visitors, employees, vendors, and medical professionals. (Policy II-U)

Boeing Airlift and Tanker

(Recipient of the Malcolm Baldrige National Quality Award)

Printed By Permission from David Spong

Operating Principles

Integrity in all we do–every action, every day

- We tell it like it is

- We will be open and candid in all our dealings

- We respect, honor, and trust one another

- We work toward consensus

- Disagreement is healthy and encouraged, but once a decision is made, we proactively support it

- We have one conversation at a time

- Our silence is consent

- We focus on issues and ideas rather than titles and personalities

- We actively listen and question to understand

- We do not attack the messenger

- We start on time, observe time limits, and structure the agenda to end on time

- We identify clear objectives and expectations for our meetings

- We have a bias for velocity

Have Fun…Enjoy the Journey and Each Other

Sharp HealthCare

(Recipient of the Malcolm Baldrige National Quality Award)

Reprinted With Permission from Sharp Healthcare

Author's Note: At Sharp the Behavior Standards are embedded everywhere, including:

- *Hallways*

- *Screen Savers*

- *Communications*

- *Meeting Discussions*

Behavior Standards

At Sharp our customers include patients, family members, physicians, co-workers, donors and volunteers, and business partners.

- **Standard #1: Attitude is Everything** *Create a Lasting Impression* We treat every customer as if he or she is the most important person in our workplace. Our behavior and attitude create a positive first impression that is lasting. We strive to exceed expectations. Immediately welcome customers with a smile, eye contact and a friendly introduction. Use open body language and a handshake. Listen with care and empathy to customers, avoid interrupting, and confirm what you have heard. Meet customers' immediate needs, or graciously take them to someone who can. Thank customers for choosing Sharp HealthCare. When asked directions, offer to escort people to their destinations, or find someone who can. Ask for help when there is a question about where the customer should be directed. Smile and say "hello" to others in hallways and elevators.

- **Standard #2: Thank Somebody** *Reward and Recognition* Reward and recognition are central to the Sharp culture. We express gratitude and appreciation to one another. We celebrate our accomplishments and hard work to make Sharp the best place to work, practice medicine, and receive care. Recognize and celebrate one another's achievements and successes. Tell someone who goes above and beyond that you appreciate him or her. Acknowledge when a team member exemplifies one or more of the service standards and behaviors. Openly praise co-workers' accomplishments.

- **Standard #3: Make Words Work** *Talk, Listen, and Learn* We communicate with courtesy, clarity, and care in all verbal and non-verbal messages. We listen attentively to customers to understand their needs and to ensure they comprehend the information we provide to them. Respond kindly to all customers with information and assistance. Ask customers what name they prefer to be called and use that name whenever possible. Answer phone calls within three rings. In a clear, friendly way, state your name and department, and ask, "How may I help you?" Acknowledge callers on hold periodically; give them the status of their calls and ask if they want to continue to hold. Avoid technical or professional jargon and acronyms. Reinforce verbal instructions with written material whenever possible. Always use "please" and "thank you," and end encounters with a courteous "good-bye."

- **Standard #4: All for One, One for All** *Teamwork* Sharp team members share a common purpose: to serve our customers. We build up each other; we share our successes, failures, information, and ideas. Communicate openly, share relevant information, and never assume. Respect the privacy of fellow employees. Treat all co-workers with courtesy and respect. Recognize that everyone has areas of expertise. Keep commitments to co-workers on assignments and meetings or communicate otherwise. Resolve conflicts respectfully, directly, and promptly with the individual(s) involved. Do not chastise or embarrass. Be tasteful and appropriate in all interactions.

- **Standard #5: Make It Better!** *Service Recovery* When the Sharp Experience doesn't go right for a customer, we pledge to make things better. We listen and respond with empathy and apologize for not exceeding expectations. We are proactive in making amends, even in difficult situations. Anticipate and correct problems before they become complaints. Listen to customers' concerns, and do not rationalize or place blame. Apologize for problems or inconveniences, even if they are not your fault. Let the customer know we will work to make things right. Initiate service recovery as warranted as a tangible acknowledgement of our commitment to service excellence.

- **Standard #6: Think Safe, Be Safe** *Safety at Work* It is essential that we provide a hospitable, healing, healthy, and safe environment at Sharp HealthCare. We identify and report safety hazards promptly, and apply remedies whenever needed. Report safety hazards immediately. Slow down and walk. Choose shoes with safety in mind.

Repair or report loose, slippery, or poorly maintained surfaces. Report burned-out light bulbs and be cautious in areas that are poorly lit. Use proper tools and equipment at all times. Follow safety procedures required for tool and equipment use. Ask for assistance and use lift equipment when appropriate. Do not take shortcuts with safety to save time. At Sharp our customers include patients, family members, physicians, co-workers, donors and volunteers, and business partners.

- **Standard #7: Look Sharp–Be Sharp** *Appearance Speaks* When we dress, groom, and maintain our workplace with care, we show respect for our customers and give them confidence in our ability to care for them. Wear neat, appropriate clothing, jewelry, and tastefully applied scents, following the organization's dress code. Wear identification badges in a visible, appropriate place. Use good personal hygiene. Keep public spaces, work areas and meeting rooms clean, clutter-free, and safe. Dispose of litter, clean up spills, and return equipment to its proper place.

- **Standard #8: Keep in Touch!** *Ease Waiting Times* Keeping our customers informed puts them and their families at ease. We are committed to sharing information and acknowledging the presence of our customers at all times. Provide a clean, comfortable atmosphere for waiting customers. Offer current, interesting, and engaging reading materials and health education videos, if possible. Contact customers, if possible, prior to the appointment if it becomes apparent that they will need to wait. Let the customer decide whether to come in later or make a new appointment, if appropriate. Educate customers about the process and expected time frames. Apologize if there is a delay, explain the reason and, if appropriate, offer options for rescheduling. Provide waiting customers with regular updates.

- **Standard #9: It's a Private Matter** *Confidentiality* Sharp HealthCare protects customers' confidentiality, privacy, and modesty in all situations. We are sensitive to the personal nature of health care, and we do everything we can to earn the trust that others place in us. We strive to promote peace of mind and relieve anxiety. Speak about personal matters in a private area or in a quiet voice. Do not discuss customers' issues in public areas. Knock and announce yourself before entering a patient room, close doors and pull curtains. Provide the proper-size gown for patients and offer a robe or covering when a patient is walking, in a wheelchair or on a gurney. When transporting a patient by elevator, do not allow the patient to be surrounded by others. Politely ask the others to wait. Be discreet in telephone conversations with or about customers. Keep patient, physician and proprietary organizational information private. Never share computer or telephone passwords or codes or leave computers unattended. Retrieve printed, copied or faxed information promptly and secure appropriately.

- **Standard #10: To "E" or not to "E"** *E-mail Manners* Using e-mail may save the sender time but may not always be the most appropriate or expedient way to communicate. Use discretion in sending, responding to, and forwarding e-mail. Remember that electronic messages can be subpoenaed and used as evidence in legal proceedings. Respond to e-mails requesting a reply within two working days. If you are gone for more than two days, use an "out of the office" message. When sending a message to multiple user groups, select only those groups to whom the message is relevant. Reply only to the sender when possible. Never correct the sender by using "reply to group." Seek approval of Corporate Communications when sending broadcast e-mail to all user groups, or to more than 50 e-mail addresses across multiple departments. Use direct communication, not e-mail, for complex problem solving, sensitive or highly confidential issues. Use priority e-mail flags only when a message is extremely important. For urgent communication, phone, or page the individual.

- **Standard #11: Vive La Différence!** *Diversity* At Sharp HealthCare, we know that our differences, unique talents, and varied backgrounds come together to create a stronger whole. Recognize the values of a diverse workforce; remain open to new viewpoints, ideas, and talents. Relate to everyone fairly, regardless of age, gender, disability, race, ethnicity, creed, national origin, religion, sexual orientation, etc. Treat all customers with respect. Provide the highest level of service to everyone.

- **Standard #12: Get Smart** *Increasing Skills and Competence* Sharp HealthCare is committed to helping its employees, leaders, and physicians learn and grow. Professional development demonstrates a desire to continually enhance the delivery of health care. We encourage innovation and constant improvement in efficiency and effectiveness. Actively participate in professional development opportunities offered by Sharp. Continually acquire new technical and computer knowledge. Maintain a high level of competence in your job, taking advantage of opportunities to learn and develop new skills. Think outside the box and contribute innovative ways of doing things.

US Air Force Core Values

Whoever you are and wherever you fit on the Air Force team, this is your basic guide to the Air Force Core Values of **Integrity first, Service before self, and Excellence in all we do**.

The Core Values exist for all members of the Air Force family: officer, enlisted, and civilian; active, reserve, and retired; senior, junior, and middle management; civil servants; uniformed personnel; and contractors. They are for all of us to read, to understand, to live by, and to cherish. The Core Values are much more than minimum standards. They remind us what it takes to get the mission done. They inspire us to do our very best at all times. They are the common bond among all comrades in arms, and they are the glue that unifies the force and ties us to the great warriors and public servants of the past. Study them, understand them, follow them, and encourage others to do the same.

Integrity First. Integrity is a character trait. It is the willingness to do what is right, even when no one is looking. It is the "moral compass," the inner voice, the voice of self-control, and the basis for the trust imperative to today's military. Integrity is the ability to hold together and properly regulate all the elements of a personality. A person of integrity, for example, is capable of acting on conviction. A person of integrity can control impulses and appetites. But integrity also covers several other moral traits indispensable to national service.

- **Courage**. A person of integrity possesses moral courage and does what is right even if the personal cost is high.

- **Honesty**. This is the hallmark of the military professional, because in the military, our word must be our bond. We don't pencil-whip training reports, we don't cover up tech data violations, we don't falsify documents, and we don't write misleading operational readiness messages. The bottom line is, we don't lie, and we can't justify any deviation from the truth.

- **Responsibility**. No person of integrity is irresponsible; a person of true integrity acknowledges his or her duties and acts accordingly.

- **Accountability**. No person of integrity tries to shift the blame to others or take credit for the work of others; "the buck stops here" says it best.

- **Justice**. A person of integrity practices justice. Those who do similar things must get similar rewards or similar punishments.

- **Openness**. Professionals of integrity encourage a free flow of information within the organization. They seek feedback from all directions to ensure they are fulfilling key responsibilities, and they are never afraid to allow anyone at any time to examine how they do business.

- **Self-respect**. To have integrity also is to respect oneself as a professional and a human being. A person of integrity does not behave in ways that would bring discredit upon himself or herself or the organization to which he or she belongs.

- **Humility**. A person of integrity grasps and is sobered by the awesome task of defending the Constitution of the United States of America.

Service before Self. Service before self tells us that professional duties take precedence over personal desires. At the very least, it includes the following behaviors.

- **Rule following**. To serve is to do one's duty, and our duties are commonly expressed through rules. While it may be the case that professionals are expected to exercise judgment in the performance of their duties, good professionals understand that rules have a reason for being, and the default position must be to follow those rules unless there is a clear, operational reason for refusing to do so.

- **Respect for others**. Service before self tells us also that a good leader places the troops ahead of his or her personal comfort. We must always act in the certain knowledge that all people possess a fundamental worth as human beings.

- **Discipline and self-control**. Professionals cannot indulge in self-pity, discouragement, anger, frustration, or defeatism. They have a fundamental moral obligation to the people they lead to strike a tone of confidence and forward-looking optimism. More specifically, they are expected to exercise control in the following areas.

- **Anger**. Military professionals and especially commanders at all echelons are expected to refrain from displays of anger that would bring discredit upon themselves and/or the Air Force.

- **Appetites.** Those who allow their appetites to drive them to make sexual overtures to subordinates are unfit for military service. Likewise, the excessive consumption of alcohol casts doubts on an individual's fitness, and if an officer is found to be drunk and disorderly, all doubts are removed.

- **Religious toleration**. Military professionals must remember that religious beliefs are a matter of individual choice. Professionals, and especially commanders, must not try to change or coercively influence the religious views of subordinates.

- **Faith in the system**. To lose faith in the system is to adopt the view that you know better than those above you in the chain of command what should or should not be done. In other words, to lose faith in the system is to place self before service. Leaders can be very influential in this regard. If a leader resists the temptation to doubt the system, then subordinates may follow suit.

Excellence in All We Do. Excellence in all we do directs us to develop a sustained passion for continual improvement and innovation that will propel the Air Force into a long-term, upward spiral of accomplishment and performance.

- **Product and service excellence**. We must focus on providing services and generating products that fully respond to customer wants and anticipate customer needs, and we must do so within the boundaries established by the taxpaying public.

- **Personal excellence**. Military professionals must seek out and complete professional military education, stay in physical and mental shape, and continue to refresh their general educational backgrounds.

- **Community excellence**. This is achieved when the members of an organization can work together to successfully reach a common goal in an atmosphere free of fear that preserves individual self-worth. Several factors influence interpersonal excellence.

- **Mutual respect.** Genuine respect involves viewing another person as an individual of fundamental worth. This means never judging a person on the basis of his or her possession of an attribute that places him or her in some racial, ethnic, economic, or gender-based category.

- **Benefit of the doubt.** Avoid making snap judgments about a person or his or her behavior; it is important to get the whole story. All coworkers should be considered innocent until proven guilty.

- **Resources excellence.** It is important to aggressively implement policies to ensure the best possible cradle-to-grave management of resources.

- **Material resources excellence.** Military professionals have an obligation to ensure that all of the equipment and property they ask for is mission essential. This means that residual funds at the end of the year should not be used to purchase "nice to have" add-ons.

- **Human resources excellence.** We should recruit, train, promote, and retain those who can do the best job for us.

- **Operations excellence.** There are two kinds of operations excellence: internal and external.

Internal operations excellence pertains to the way we do business internal to the Air Force, from the unit level to Headquarters Air

Force. It involves respect on the unit level and a total commitment to maximizing the Air Force team effort.

External operations excellence pertains to the way we treat the world around us as we conduct our operations. In peacetime we must be sensitive to the rules governing environmental pollution, for example, and in wartime we are required to obey the laws of war.

Why These Core Values? Core Values make the military what it is; without them, we cannot succeed. They are the values that instill confidence, earn lasting respect, and create willing followers. They are the values that anchor resolve in the most difficult situations. They are the values that buttress mental and physical courage when we enter combat. In essence, they are the three pillars of professionalism that provide the foundation for military leadership at every level. With the incredible diversity of our organization and the myriad of functions necessary to make it work efficiently and effectively, Core Values remain unifying elements for all our members. They provide a common ground and compass by which we can all measure our ideals and actions. —Former Secretary of the Air Force Dr. Sheila E. Widnall

There are **four reasons** why we recognize the Core Values and have developed a strategy to implement them.

First, the Core Values tell us the price of admission to the Air Force itself. Air Force personnel—whether officer, enlisted, civil servant, or contractor—must display honesty, courage, responsibility, openness, self-respect, and humility in the face of the mission. All of us must accept accountability and practice justice, which means that all Air Force personnel must possess integrity first. At the same time, the individual's desires must take a backseat to Air Force service. Rules must be acknowledged and followed faithfully; other personnel must be respected as persons of fundamental worth; discipline and self-control must be in effect always; and there must be faith in the system. In other words, the price of admission to the Air Force demands that each of us place service before self. And it is imperative that we all seek excellence in all we do, whether it be product and service, resources, community, or operations excellence.

Second, the Core Values point to what is universal and unchanging in the profession of arms. Some are bothered by the fact that different branches of the service recognize different values; other people are bothered by the fact that the Air Force once recognized six values and has now reduced them to three. But they need not worry. It is impossible for three or six or nine Core Values to capture the richness that is at the heart of the profession of arms. The values are road signs inviting us to consider key features of the requirements of professional service, but they cannot hope to point out everything. By examining integrity, service, and excellence, we also eventually discover the importance of duty, honor, country, dedication, fidelity, competence, and a host of other professional requirements and attributes. The important thing is not the three road signs our leaders choose; what is important is that they have selected road signs, and it is our obligation to understand the ethical demands these road signs place upon us.

Third, the Core Values help us get a feel for the ethical climate of the organization. How successful are we in trying to live by the Core Values? Our answer to this question may not be the one we'd like to give. All of us have heard about the sensational scandals—senior officers and NCOs engaged in adulterous fraternization; the exchange of acquisition information for post–Air Force employment; issues like prisoner abuse in Iraq; or sexual assault upon any person, male or female. We all have read about these incidents and experienced the shame associated with them. But these big-ticket scandals don't just happen in a vacuum, and they aren't always caused by evil people acting on impulse. The people involved knew the difference between right and wrong, and they knew what professionalism demanded in these situations. These scandals grew out of a climate of ethical erosion. Because we believe our operating procedures or the requirements levied upon us from above are absurd, we tend to cut corners, skate by, and get over. As time goes by, these actions become easier and even habitual, until one day we can no longer distinguish between the important taskings or rules and the stupid ones. Lying on official forms becomes second nature. Placing personal interests ahead of the mission seems sensible. And we develop a "good enough for government work" mentality. In such a climate of corrosion, the Core Values are like a slap in the face. How far have you strayed from integrity, service, and excellence? What about the folks with whom you work?

Fortunately, there is a **fourth** reason for recognizing the Core Values. Just as they help us evaluate the climate of our organization, they also serve as beacons to keep us on the path of correct professional conduct. The Core Values allow us to transform a climate of ethical erosion into one of ethical commitment. That is why we have developed the Core Values Strategy.

The Core Values Strategy

1. The Core Values Strategy exists independently of and does not compete with chapel programs. The Core Values Strategy attempts no explanation of the origin of the Values except to say that all of us, regardless of our religious views, must recognize their functional importance and accept them for that reason. Infusing the Core Values is necessary for successful mission accomplishment.

2. You don't need to be a commander in order to be a leader.

3. The leader of an organization is the key to its moral climate. As does the commander, so does the organization. But a commander must enlist and insist upon the help of all organizational supervisors and all assigned personnel in the effort to ensure a culture of conscience for the organization.

4. Leaders cannot just be good; they also must be sensitive to their status as role models for their people and thus avoid the appearance of improper behavior.

5. Leadership from below is at least as important as leadership from above in implementing the Core Values.

6. A culture of conscience is impossible unless civilians, officers, and enlisted personnel understand, accept, internalize, and are free to follow the Core Values.

7. To understand, accept, and internalize the Core Values, our people must be allowed and encouraged to engage in an extended dialogue about them and to explore the role of the Values at all levels of the Air Force.

8. Our first task is to fix organizations; individual character development is possible, but it is not a goal. If a culture of compromise exists in the Air Force, it is more likely to be the result of bad policies and programs than to be symptomatic of any character flaws in our people. Therefore, long before we seek to implement a character development program, we must thoroughly evaluate and, where necessary, fix our policies, processes, and procedures.

Further information on the Values can be found at the U.S. Air Force's e-Publishing website, which contains a copy of The Little Blue Book:

www.e-publishing.af.mil/shared/media/document/AFD-070906-003.pdf

The "Our Values" section of the Air Force website (www.airforce.com/learn-about/our-values) also has a feature by which you may submit questions about the Core Values.

REQUIREMENT FOR EXEMPLARY CONDUCT All commanding officers and others in authority in the Air Force are required by §10 USC 8583 of the U.S. Code

- to show in themselves a good example of virtue, honor, patriotism, and subordination;

- to be vigilant in inspecting the conduct of all persons who are placed under their command;

- to guard against and suppress all dissolute and immoral practices, and to correct, according to the laws and regulations of the Air Force, all persons who are guilty of them; and

- to take all necessary and proper measures, under the laws, regulations, and customs of the Air Force, to promote and safeguard the morale, the physical well-being, and the general welfare of the officers and enlisted persons under their command or charge.

Teamwork. Teamwork is the means by which officers do the impossible more rapidly. Teamwork makes football champions of eleven people who, if they all insisted on being ball carriers, would gain nothing. Teamwork makes every officer's task easier, and yet the overall result is greater success. It is the nearest thing to getting something for nothing. If you insist on playing a lone hand, always want to carry the ball, and feel that associates should do their own work without bothering you, you will find that your path is rough and does not go very far. Cooperation with others is essential, as the Air Force is a team organization.

Adaptability. One of the qualities that Air Force officers must employ the most is adaptability, the ability to make the best of any situation. Life in the Air Force is a rough-and-tumble of widely varying conditions. Officers serve in all parts of the world, in an almost infinite number of differing conditions. Equipment and technology change frequently, new maintenance problems arise, and all things are subject to change. As an officer, you must be prepared to adapt to the conditions you may find in any assignment. Living accommodations, offices, operational facilities, the quality of superiors and subordinates—all may differ radically from your previous assignment, yet you must work with these new factors. You, not they, must adapt. Adaptability and flexibility are essential to meet such different situations.

Sense of Responsibility. Responsibility is one of the most valued characteristics in an officer. Its most frequent evidence is the execution of work that should be done whether you are directly charged with that work. How many times can you hear the phrase from the substandard officer: "Oh, well, it's not my headache"? But it is your headache if it hurts the Air Force. The sense of responsibility found in the best of Air Force officers will not be satisfied with a job merely well done. The question is: Has the job been done to the best of my ability? If not, it isn't finished.

Coaching And Coaching Philosophy – The Great Coaches

John Wooden

John Wooden was one of the most successful and influential coaches in the history of basketball. Here's a summary of his coaching philosophy:

Pyramid of Success

Wooden's famous "Pyramid of Success" outlines the building blocks he felt were necessary to achieve winning and success, both on and off the court. The pyramid's foundational blocks include industriousness, friendship, loyalty, cooperation, and enthusiasm. The higher blocks focus on self-control, alertness, initiative, intentness, condition, skill, team spirit, poise, and confidence-- culminating in competitive greatness at the pyramid's peak.

Fundamentals and Preparation

Wooden was a stickler for mastering the fundamentals and basics of the game through continuous drilling and preparation. His teams spent countless hours perfecting footwork, ball-handling, shooting, defense and conditioning. He believed flawless execution of the basics was the key to winning.

Character and Leadership

Beyond just basketball skills, Wooden placed a heavy emphasis on building character, values, and leadership in his players. He taught them life lessons about determination, perseverance, self-discipline and being a humble, respectful team player. Cultivating these intangibles was vital.

Full Effort

Wooden demanded his players always give their full effort, whether in practice or games. He preached "failing to prepare is preparing to fail" and insisted on everyone going all-out. Half-speed or lazy play was unacceptable. Maximum effort was required.

Team Over Self

While he developed individual skills, Wooden's philosophy centered on selfless players committed to the team over personal glory. Moving without the ball, defensive intensity, and team chemistry were paramount.

His wisdom, simple yet profound messages, and ability to instill his principles in players made Wooden one of the greatest coaches and leaders in all domains of sports.

Vince Lombardi

A summary of Vince Lombardi's legendary coaching philosophy:

Commitment to Excellence

Lombardi's core tenet was a relentless pursuit of excellence in everything his teams did. He demanded complete effort, preparation and dedication from his players and coaching staff. His famous quote--"We will chase perfection, and we will chase it relentlessly" --exemplified this mindset.

Mastering the Fundamentals

Lombardi believed strongly in teaching and drilling the fundamental skills and basics of football repeatedly until they became habit. He started from the very fundamentals like blocking and tackling each season, no matter how successful the previous year.

Mental Toughness

He instilled a blue-collar, hard-nosed mental toughness in his players, pushing them to play through pain, adversity, and exhaustion. Lombardi wanted teams that were disciplined and willing to outwork and outhit opponents through sheer force of will.

Teamwork and Sacrifice

While creating tremendous individual motivation, Lombardi's system emphasized the supremacy of the team over individual stars. He demanded cohesion, selflessness and players being willing to sacrifice personal stats for team success.

Responsibility and Accountability

Lombardi held himself and his players strictly accountable. He created an atmosphere of shared responsibility where there were no excuses for mistakes or failure. Everyone had to take ownership.

Dignity, Pride and Confidence

The coach aimed to instill immense dignity, pride, and self-confidence in his players both on and off the field through his leadership and lofty expectations. Belief and class were essential.

With his intensity, incredible motivation skills and ability to raise his players' mental toughness to championship levels, Lombardi's philosophy became the gold standard in professional coaching.

Lou Holtz

A summary of Lou Holtz's coaching philosophy:

Positive Attitude

Holtz believed strongly in always maintaining a positive attitude and optimistic mindset. He felt negativity bred more negativity, so he constantly pushed his players to have an upbeat, can-do approach.

Value of Hard Work

One of Holtz's core principles was that success comes through hard work, discipline and dedication--there are no shortcuts. He instilled a blue-collar work ethic in his teams through grueling practices and attention to detail.

Overcoming Adversity

Holtz emphasized always giving maximum effort and never quitting, no matter the obstacles or adversity faced. He taught his players to persevere, fight through setbacks and find ways to overcome challenges.

Teaching Life Lessons

While focused on winning, Holtz also used football as a vehicle to teach larger life lessons about integrity, accountability, sacrifice and being a good person off the field. Character-building was essential.

Motivational Tactics

Holtz was a master motivator who used fiery speeches, bold statements, creative gimmicks, and reverse psychology to inspire and push his players to new heights of performance.

Trust and Loyalty

He stressed the importance of trust between coaches and players, never misleading them. Holtz also engendered fierce loyalty by demonstrating his own commitment to the program.

With his relentless positivity, ability to motivate and focus on building men of character, Lou Holtz's holistic coaching approach led to great success at several programs.

Pat Riley

A summary of Pat Riley's coaching philosophy:

The Disease of Me

Riley strongly believed that individual agendas and selfishness were a "disease" that could destroy a team. He preached that players must subjugate their egos and personal stats for the greater good of the team's success.

No Excuses

Riley had a "No Excuses" mentality and demanded his players take full accountability. He would not tolerate blaming officials, injuries, or any other factors as excuses for poor performance.

Conditioning and Preparation

He was renowned for having some of the most intense, grueling practice regimens focused on conditioning. Riley believed superior preparation and effort in practice carried over to games.

Mental Toughness

Riley aimed to instill incredible mental toughness in his teams through challenging them physically and mentally every day. He wanted players who could remain poised under pressure.

Motivation Tactics

He used motivational ploys like the infamous "Armani Suits" and other mind games to light a fire under complacent players when needed.

Defensive Identity

While having talented offensive players, Riley's teams prided themselves on tenacious, swarming defensive intensity that took away opponents' strengths.

Never coddling egos and pushing his players to maximize their conditioning and mental toughness defined Riley's hardnosed approach that led to multiple NBA championships with the "ShowTime" Lakers and Miami Heat teams.

Glossary

Key Terms

Most of this glossary was taken directly from the Baldrige Criteria (NIST, 2019–2020, pp 46-53). The definitions have been slightly edited, and some definitions added for use with this workbook.

Where the term being defined is in italics the italicized part of the definition has been provided by the author and is not endorsed by the Malcolm Baldrige National Quality Award Office.

Action Plans

The term "action plans" refers to specific actions that respond to short- and longer-term strategic objectives. Action plans include details of resource commitments and time horizons for accomplishment. Action plan development represents the critical stage in planning when strategic objectives and goals are made specific so that effective, organization-wide understanding, and deployment are possible. In the Criteria, deployment of action plans includes creating aligned measures for all departments and work units. Deployment also might require specialized training for some employees or recruitment of personnel.

An example of a strategic objective for a supplier in a highly competitive industry might be to develop and maintain a price leadership position. Action plans could entail designing efficient processes and creating an accounting system that tracks activity-level costs, aligned for the organization as a whole. Deployment requirements might include work unit and team training in setting priorities based on costs and benefits. Organizational-level analysis and review likely would emphasize productivity growth, cost control, and quality.

Analysis

The term "analysis" refers to an examination of facts and data to provide a basis for effective decisions. Analysis often involves the determination of cause-effect relationships. Overall organizational analysis guides the management of work systems and work processes toward achieving key business results and toward attaining strategic objectives. Despite their importance, individual facts and data do not usually provide an effective basis for actions or setting priorities. Effective actions depend on an understanding of relationships, derived from analysis of facts and data.

Balancing Value

A key challenge to an organization will frequently include balancing the differing expectations of the various stakeholder groups. To meet the sometimes conflicting and changing aims that balancing value implies, organizational strategy (normally in the environmental scan phase of strategy development) should explicitly include key stakeholder requirements. This will help the organization develop strategies (and the associated plans and actions) which are aligned to maximize the overall stakeholder benefit, and to achieve what the leaders of the organization intended to achieve.

This does not mean that all stakeholders will get anything they want. It does mean that the leadership needs to start with the stakeholder requirements and determine the most effective/innovative way to serve the needs of multiple stakeholders. During the planning the balance intended by the leaders (between the stakeholder requirements and how they will/will not be met) should be linked to the beliefs of the organization (e.g., mission, vision, values), and the needs of the multiple stakeholders The balanced intended should be the balance planned, the balance resourced, the balance deployed, the balance reviewed (during performance reviews), and the balance achieved.

Behavior

The term "behavior" refers to how an individual acts or the actions taken in a given situation. This area is one where leaders must define the expected, desired, or mandatory behaviors. These are typically a translation of the Vision, Mission, Values (which are beliefs) into actions.

Once defined leaders must not equivocate on the adherence to the established behaviors. Within an organization what is condoned is endorsed by the leader.

Blind Spot

The term "blind spot" refers to an area which is not being addressed by the organization, which is an obscuration of the visual field (or environmental scan) during the planning and implementation of actions. A particular blind spot is the place in the "visual" field which is not being addressed. If an organization does not address a blind spot, there is some level of risk to the organization or to organizational performance–a blind spot is something that could potentially interfere with organizational performance and strategy.

Blind spots can be something the organization is unaware of, something they are aware of, or even something they understand. In any event, however, a decision to act to remove or mitigate the blind spot has not been made, and actions have not been taken.

Once a decision to act is made, the organization should monitor the progress of the actions to determine whether the intended effect of removing or mitigating the risk has occurred. If action is not taken, the organization may still want to monitor the blind spot to ensure the level of risk, which the blind spot represents, does not change to an unacceptable level.

For example, known blind spots can be areas which the organization is aware of, but they have not taken action to mitigate the risk because of a conscious leadership decision that the risk is acceptable. Additionally, some known blind spots can be of a nature that the organization does not know what to do about them or cannot do anything about them.

Unknown blind spots are areas of risk the organization is not aware of. Frequently these are addressed with the use of specific external experts who can make the organization aware of risks that were previously unknown.

Core Competencies

The term "core competencies" refers to your organization's areas of greatest expertise. Your organization's core competencies are those strategically important capabilities that are central to fulfilling your mission or provide an advantage in your marketplace or service environment. Core competencies frequently are challenging for competitors or suppliers and partners to imitate, and they may provide a sustainable competitive advantage. Core competencies may involve technology expertise, unique service offerings, a marketplace niche, or business acumen (e.g., business acquisitions).

Culture

The set of customs, traditions, values, and behaviors of an organization or community. Culture is reflected in the behavior norms which are defined and known, promoted, allowed, or condoned. In an organization with a strong/well deployed culture, the members of the organization know the culture, and behave accordingly. To not do so would typically mean the individual does not fit in the organization and will not (typically) be allowed to stay.

Customer

The term "customer" refers to actual and potential users of your organization's products, programs, or services (referred to as "products" in the Criteria). Customers include the end users of your products, as well as others who might be their immediate purchasers or users. These others might include distributors, agents, or organizations that further process your product as a component of their product. The Criteria address customers broadly, referencing current and future customers, as well as the customers of your competitors.

Customer Engagement

The term "customer engagement" refers to your customers' investment in or commitment to your brand and product offerings. It is based on your ongoing ability to serve their needs and build relationships so they will continue using your products. Characteristics of customer engagement include customer retention and loyalty, customers' willingness to try to do business with your organization, and customers' willingness to actively advocate for and recommend your brand and product offerings.

Effective

The term "effective" refers to how well a process or a measure addresses its intended purpose. Determining effectiveness requires (1) the evaluation of how well the process is aligned with the organization's needs and how well the process is deployed or (2) the evaluation of the outcome of the measure used.

Embedded Core Belief

A term used by some organizations to describe the one belief which is so key it is at the top of every thought, process, plan, measure, and action. This is part of an organization's DNA. This is beyond core values. This helps give an organization a singular focus on something which is key to their short- and longer-term survivability or differentiation.

For example–survivability: in a heavy industrial environment, an embedded core belief might be safety. To violate this could mean loss of life in the factory.

For example–differentiation: in a business which is not typically known for honest business dealings --the organization could differentiate themselves with "integrity" as an embedded core belief. To violate this could mean loss of brand image and differentiation in the marketplace.

An embedded core belief is, typically, an area where very little, if any, empowerment is given. Organizational members do not consciously violate the embedded core belief and stay with the organization. If this intentionally happens, the disconnect between the organizational beliefs and a personal behavior would be too great.

Ethical Behavior–Role Model

The term "ethical behavior" refers to how an organization ensures that all its decisions, actions, and stakeholder interactions conform to the organization's moral and professional principles. These principles should support all applicable laws and regulations and are the foundation for the organization's culture and values. They distinguish "right" from "wrong."

Senior leaders should act as role models for these principles of behavior. The principles apply to all people involved in the organization, from temporary members of the workforce to members of the board of directors and need to be communicated and reinforced on a regular basis. Although there is no universal model for ethical behavior, senior leaders should ensure that the organization's mission and vision are aligned with its ethical principles. Ethical behavior should be practiced with all stakeholders, including the workforce, shareholders, customers, partners, suppliers, and the organization's local community.

While some organizations may view their ethical principles as boundary conditions restricting behavior, well-designed and clearly articulated ethical principles should empower people to make effective decisions with great confidence.

Goals

The term "goals" refers to a future condition or performance level that one intends to attain. Goals can be both short- and longer-term. Goals are ends that guide actions. Quantitative goals, frequently referred to as "targets," include a numerical point or range. Targets might be projections based on comparative or competitive data. The term "stretch goals" refers to desired major, discontinuous (non-incremental) or "breakthrough" improvements, usually in areas most critical to your organization's future success.

High Performance

Ever-higher levels of overall organizational and individual performance, including quality, productivity, innovation rate, and cycle time. High performance results in improved service and value for customers and other stakeholders.

Approaches to high performance vary in their form, their function, and the incentive systems used. High performance stems from and enhances workforce engagement. It involves cooperation between the management and the workforce, which may involve workforce bargaining units; cooperation among work units, often involving teams; empowerment of your people, including personal accountability; and workforce input into planning. It may involve learning and building individual and organizational skills; learning from other organizations; creating flexible job design and work assignments; maintaining a flattened organizational structure, where decision making is decentralized and decisions are made closest to the front line; and effectively using performance measures, including comparisons. Many organizations encourage high performance with monetary and nonmonetary incentives based on factors such as organizational performance, team and individual contributions, and skill building. Also, approaches to high performance usually seek to align your organization's structure, core competencies, work, jobs, workforce development, and incentives.

Innovation

The term "innovation" refers to making meaningful change to improve products, processes, or organizational effectiveness and to create new value for stakeholders. Innovation involves the adoption of an idea, process, technology, product, or business model that is either new or new to its proposed application. The outcome of innovation is a discontinuous or breakthrough change in results, products, or processes.

Successful organizational innovation is a multistep process that involves development and knowledge sharing, a decision to implement, implementation, evaluation, and learning. Although innovation is often associated with technological innovation, it is applicable to all key organizational processes that would benefit from change, whether through breakthrough improvement or a change in approach or outputs. It could include fundamental changes in organizational structure or the business model to accomplish the organization's work more effectively.

Leadership System

The term "leadership system" refers to how leadership is exercised, formally and informally, throughout the organization; it is the basis for and the way key decisions are made, communicated, and carried out. It includes structures and mechanisms for decision making; two-way communication; selection and development of leaders and managers; and reinforcement of values, ethical behavior, directions, and performance expectations.

An effective leadership system respects the capabilities and requirements of workforce members and other stakeholders, and it sets high expectations for performance and performance improvement. It builds loyalties and teamwork based on the organization's vision and values and the pursuit of shared goals. It encourages and supports initiative and appropriate risk taking, it subordinates organizational structure to purpose and function, and avoids chains of command that require long decision paths. An effective leadership system includes mechanisms for the leaders to conduct self-examination, receive feedback, and improve.

The term "leader," as it is used in reference to the Leadership System, refers to all leaders at any level in the organization. This is not only limited to the top leaders (the head of the organization and that person's direct reports–which are referred to as "Senior Leadership") but includes every leader supervising at least one other person. In some organizations key positions are considered leaders even if they do not supervise, and in other organizations all employees are considered leaders.

Measures and Indicators

The term "measures and indicators" refers to numerical information that quantifies input, output, and performance dimensions of processes, products, programs, projects, services, and the overall organization (outcomes). Measures and indicators might be simple (derived from one measurement) or composite.

The Criteria do not make a distinction between measures and indicators. However, some users of these terms prefer "indicator" (1) when the measurement relates to performance but is not a direct measure of such performance (e.g., the number of complaints is an indicator of dissatisfaction but not a direct measure of it) and (2) when the measurement is a predictor ("leading indicator") of some more significant performance (e.g., increased customer satisfaction might be a leading indicator of market share gain).

Mission

The term "mission" refers to the overall function of an organization. The mission answers the question, "What is this organization attempting to accomplish?" The mission might define customers or markets served, distinctive or core competencies, or technologies used.

Performance

The term "performance" refers to outputs and their outcomes obtained from processes, products, and customers that permit evaluation and comparison relative to goals, standards, past results, and other organizations. Performance can be expressed in nonfinancial and financial terms.

Performance Excellence

The term "performance excellence" refers to an integrated approach to organizational performance management that results in (1) delivery of ever-improving value to customers and stakeholders, contributing to organizational sustainability; (2) improvement of overall organizational effectiveness and capabilities; and (3) organizational and personal learning. The Baldrige Criteria for Performance Excellence provide a framework and an assessment tool for understanding organizational strengths and opportunities for improvement and thus for guiding planning efforts.

Process

Linked activities with the purpose of producing a product (or service) for a customer (user) within or outside your organization. Generally, processes involve combinations of people, machines, tools, techniques, materials, and improvements in a defined series of steps or actions. Processes rarely operate in isolation and must be considered in relation to other processes that impact them. In some situations, processes might require adherence to a specific sequence of steps, with documentation (sometimes formal) of procedures and requirements, including well-defined measurement and control steps.

In the delivery of services, particularly those that directly involve customers, process is used more generally to spell out what delivering that service entails, possibly including a preferred or expected sequence. If a sequence is critical, the process needs to include information that helps customers understand and follow the sequence. Such service processes also require guidance for service providers on handling contingencies related to customers' possible actions or behaviors.

Results

Outputs and outcomes achieved by your organization in addressing the requirements of a Baldrige Criteria Item. Results are evaluated on the basis of current performance; performance relative to appropriate comparisons; the rate, breadth, and importance of performance improvements; and the relationship of results measures to key organizational performance requirements. For further description, see the Scoring System.

Root Cause and/or Root Cause Analysis

A "root cause" is defined as a factor which truly causes a problem.

Many times, to solve a problem people will address the most visible cause which can usually be called a "symptom" of the problem.

Root cause analysis (commonly called an RCA) is an analytical approach to determine what really is causing the problem, with the objective of permanently correcting the problem. If the actual root cause is found and corrected, the problem will go away. If the root cause is not addressed, and only a symptom is corrected, the problem typically reoccurs.

The action taken from the RCA needs to be systematic and hardwired so all who use the components of the solution know the correct actions to be taken not to reestablish the problem.

Stakeholders

The term "stakeholders" refers to all groups that are or might be affected by an organization's actions and success. Examples of key stakeholders might include customers, the workforce, partners, collaborators, governing boards, stockholders, donors, suppliers, taxpayers, regulatory bodies, policy makers, funders, and local and professional communities.

See also the definition of "customer."

Systematic

The term "systematic" refers to approaches that are well-ordered, are repeatable, and use data and information so learning is possible. In other words, approaches are systematic if they build in the opportunity for evaluation, improvement, and sharing, thereby permitting a gain in maturity.

Systematic Process

A systematic process, typically, is a process where the steps undertaken are:

- **Defined**--how the organization does something (the steps are defined to a level where all parties involved and/or outsiders can understand the sequence of activities, who is involved, and what happens in each step).

- **Measured**--each of the steps has measures (these can be in-process measures or end-of -process measures) --which indicate whether steps and/or the entire process is on track.

- **Stabilized**--this means that each step of the process and/or the entire process is reliable or repeatable and can give consistent results to the organization.

- **Improved**–each of the processes has improvement and feedback cycles (where each time you go through the process there is a learning cycle which can be used at the beginning of that process the next time it is repeated).

Values

The term "values" refers to the guiding principles and behaviors that embody how your organization and its people are expected to operate. Values reflect and reinforce the desired culture of an organization. Values support and guide the decision making of every workforce member, helping the organization accomplish its mission and attain its vision in an appropriate manner. Examples of values might include demonstrating integrity and fairness in all interactions, exceeding customer expectations, valuing individuals and diversity, protecting the environment, and striving for performance excellence every day.

Vision

The term "vision" refers to the desired future state of your organization. The vision describes where the organization is headed, what it intends to be, or how it wishes to be perceived in the future.

Workforce

The term "workforce" refers to all people actively involved in accomplishing the work of your organization, including paid employees (e.g., permanent, part-time, temporary, and telecommuting employees, as well as contract employees supervised by the organization) and volunteers, as appropriate. The workforce includes team leaders, supervisors, and managers at all levels.

> *"Be the change you hope to see in the world."*
> *Mahatma Gandhi*

About the Author

Walt Carter

With more than twenty-five years in technology leadership roles, Walt specializes in change leadership, value delivery, and innovation.

Walt delivered digital transformations at Generation Mortgage, Primary Capital Mortgage, and Homestar Financial Services. He and his teams have been highlighted in major press and have received accolades from the New York Times, the Wall Street Journal, Kiplinger's, Bloomberg and MarketWatch for innovative use of technology as key differentiators for his companies.

Walt is adept at working through complex business challenges and has successfully implemented many enterprise-wide packaged software solutions for companies with global footprints. Walt is a polished professional speaker and author on the topics of change leadership and using culture as a lever for optimization.

After earning a BS in Physics from Guilford College, he began his career as a technical officer in the US Air Force supporting nuclear weapons systems and serving in very challenging Cold War assignments as a logistics planner and strategist while earning an MSA in Public and Private Administration. Since then, he has served in a variety of technology leadership roles with companies such as Fidelity, Gannett, BDM, and TRW. While at TRW, he won the President's Award for his leadership on their largest commercial project at Delta Airlines. Walt has enjoyed learning and coaching inside organizations as a Chief Operating Officer, Chief Information Officer and as a Chief Marketing Officer. One of the first to hold the Chief Digital Officer title, he brings a "team sports" philosophy to every role.

In 2020, Walt was named to the Constellation Research "Business Transformation 150" – a global list recognizing transformational leadership in the Chief Digital Officer role at Homestar. His first book on change leadership, "We Can't Stay Here!" is an international best seller.

Walt is currently serving as President and COO for THG Advisors, a division of Alba International Services and is a venture partner with Big Sky Capital.

Mr. Carter currently serves as a board advisor for QualiZeal, RK Tech, NetServ Applications, and Apex Assemblies.

John Vinyard

Managing Partner and Co-Founder of Genitect, an organizational diagnosis, design, and transformation firm with offices in Atlanta and New York.

Worked with numerous clients in the US and Europe, the Middle East, India, Asia and the Pacific Rim. He specializes in working with leadership teams to help transform their organizations. He has worked with 17 Baldrige recipients, including:

- Greater Baltimore Medical Center (2019 Baldrige Recipient)

- Don Chalmers Ford (2016 Baldrige Recipient)

- Charleston Area Medical Center (2015 Baldrige Recipient)

- Pewaukee School System (2013 Baldrige Recipient)

- Baylor Regional Medical Center, Plano (Announced as a 2013 recipient)

- Advocate Good Samaritan Hospital (2010 Baldrige Recipient)

- VA Cooperative Studies Program Clinical Research Pharmacy Coordinating Center (2009 Baldrige Recipient)

- Poudre Valley Health System (2008 Baldrige Recipient)

- Sharp Healthcare (2007 Baldrige Recipient)

- Northern Mississippi Medical Center (2006 Baldrige Recipient)

- PRO-TEC Coating Company (2007 Baldrige Recipient)

- Monfort School of Business, University of Northern Colorado (2004 Baldrige Recipient)

- Boeing Aerospace (2003 Baldrige Recipient)

- Clarke American (2001 Baldrige Recipient)

- Ritz Carlton Hotel Company (1999 Baldrige Recipient)

- Boeing Airlift & Tanker (1998 Baldrige Recipient)

- Corning Telecommunications Products Division (1995 Baldrige Recipient).

John has worked with over 25 health care clients, and the U.S. Army, U.S. Air Force, Eaton Corporation, Lanier Worldwide, Cessna Aircraft, Shorts Brothers LLC, TATA Sons Ltd. (over 20 different divisions - India), InfoSys (India), Bekaert Corporation (Belgium – the first recipient of the European Foundation for Quality Management (EFQM) Award), and many others.

John is licensed by the Federal Aviation Administration (FAA) in Airframe and Powerplant Maintenance.

John was on the Board of Directors of Navicent Healthcare System, Macon, Georgia.

He has held positions as:

- Director, Engine Maintenance, United Airlines

- VP Quality and Manufacturing Operations, GenCorp Polymer Products

- Group VP, Manufacturing, Cadmus Communications

- President and CEO of Bekaert Associates, Inc.

- His first job was as a Quality Engineer for Pratt & Whitney Aircraft

Awards Include:

- **Distinguished Achievement Award**- Los Angeles Council of Engineers and Scientists

- **Fellow (FIAE)** - The Institute for the Advancement of Engineering

- **Distinguished Interprofessional Engineering Achievement Award** - Society of Professional Engineers

- **Distinguished Productivity Engineering Achievement Award** - California Council of Industrial and Business Associations

www.ingramcontent.com/pod-product-compliance
Lightning Source LLC
Chambersburg PA
CBHW021608120626
46545CB00001B/124